LOOP, ROLL, AND KEEP CONTROL

HIGH FLIGHT
P U B L I S H I N G

Loop, Roll, and Keep Control – A Step-By-Step Aerobatic, Spin, and Upset Manual

Published by High Flight Publishing LLC™

Minneapolis, Minnesota

Copyright 2020 by James Luger, Minnesota, USA. All rights reserved.

ISBN: 978-1-7330982-2-9 (Paperback)

This book is also available as an e-book, ISBN: 978-1-7330982-3-6

A CIP catalogue record for this title is available from the Library of Congress.

This High Flight Publishing paperback edition published 2020.

WARNING: Do not attempt any aerobatic maneuver without flight instruction from a qualified aerobatic certified flight instructor, and do not perform aerobatic maneuvers solo unless your instructor advises that you are competent to perform specific maneuvers safely, and that you are competent to identify and correct errors associated with each maneuver.

Trademarks: High Flight Publishing™ and the High Flight Publishing logo.

Printed in the United States of America

Interior Illustrations by Arland Nau

Interior Design by Lin White

Cover Design by Jessica Bell

The photographic image of an Xtreme Decathlon on the cover is provided with permission from American Champion Aircraft Corporation.

Loop, Roll, and Keep Control

A Step-By-Step Aerobatic, Spin, and Upset Manual

By Jim Luger

Illustrations by Arland Nau

Also by Jim Luger, a novel

Lost in Dalat – The Courage of a Family Torn by War

When a woman searches for the Vietnam battlefield where her missing-in-action father was long ago last seen alive, she uncovers mysterious secrets about him, secrets that now threaten her life.

"I read page one and stayed up all night. I couldn't put the damn thing down!"

—Larry Stoller (Minnesota USA)

Learn more at **JamesLuger.com**

If Your Airplane Falls Out of the Sky

• The worst place for a surprise

While climbing out on the crosswind leg during a flight review, I once asked a pilot "What would you do right now if a wing dipped into a spin?" While turning downwind, he mumbled something about right rudder. During the ground portion of his flight review, I talked about spin recoveries and the upset maneuver training you'll soon be reading about in this book.

• What just happened?

Every now and then a beginning aerobatic student, prior to any spin training, will inadvertently enter a stall or spin during a high angle of attack (AOA) or high G-load maneuver. The reaction of the student is often bewilderment, and sometimes loss of control. Even if I don't need to take the controls, an error like that gives me an opportunity to make a case for the spin and aerobatic training discussed in this book.

• Getting flipped

An unintended rollover to inverted during normal operations is rare (although it's happened to me twice—more about that later), but whenever I've asked a non-aerobatic pilot what he would do if he suddenly found himself in an inverted dive, perhaps just past knife edge, the response is typically something between "Ah…well…[*crickets*]" to "I'd pull it out of the dive." Neither response bodes well for a safe recovery, but you'll soon learn how to easily recover from unintended inverted dives.

Yes, those things can really happen, and here's the proof...

My decades of advocacy for spin and aerobatic training is reinforced by the analysis of general aviation accident statistics in the periodic Joseph T. Nall Report, which is available from the Aircraft Owners and Pilots Association (AOPA) Air Safety Institute. These statistics show that a high number of general aviation airplane accidents result from stalls and spins, often at low altitude, many of them fatal. Statistics, however, do not always explain the chain of ignored errors—such as extreme attitudes, cross-controlling, airspeed and AOA neglect, and energy mismanagement— that can quickly lead to stalls, spins, and loss of control. The mission of this book is to be your primary knowledge handbook for flight training that will help you recognize those errors early, and either prevent them or recover quickly from any mishaps.

And now the fun part

I don't want this stressful introduction to ruin the fun you have flying merrily along from airport A to airport B—in fact, I want to increase your fun and decrease your stress. That's why I hope you enjoy reading this book for new knowledge, and then use what you learn to acquire new skills with some basic aerobatic, spin, and upset flight training. You'll discover how exciting and fun flying can really be, and you'll be rewarded by feeling more in command of your airplane.

— Jim Luger

Contents

Loop, Roll, and Keep Control

A Step-By-Step Aerobatic, Spin, and Upset Manual

Introduction to Taming Your Airplane

Before I teach pilots how to recover from mishaps and upsets, I make sure they learn at least some aerobatic and spin skills. Here's why.

I've been flipped upside down twice in my flying career, once in a Cessna 172 from wake turbulence while on short final behind a C-130 military transport plane, and once in a Super Cub on floats in Alaska from a sudden down-gust while flying along the lee side of a mountain pass. Both events rolled me just past knife edge. In case you didn't know, rolling past knife edge is inverted, so pulling back on the stick would have made me go down. But I didn't go down.

Instead, I recovered instantly with basic aerobatic moves. I pushed on the stick to maintain altitude while inverted, and simultaneously made a coordinated half-roll back to upright. In each incident I recovered in about three seconds with negligible altitude loss. Without prior aerobatic training, however, I would not have had time to sort out a recovery for what is officially and ominously called *"Loss of control in flight."*

There was no time for aeronautical decision-making (ADM)

ADM sequence charts are helpful to follow if you have sufficient time and altitude for a step-by-step decision chain, but for the above upsets, an intuitive snap decision and correct automatic action was critical. Of course, that decisive action was based on prior aerobatic and upset training, where ADM was taught on the ground, and is an important theme in this book's curriculum. But while knowledge can be gained by reading, upset recovery skills require practice in the air under the professional guidance of an aerobatic certified flight instructor. Combining knowledge and flight training will help you learn an important new aviation skillset that could someday save you and your passengers.

Is everyday flying really that dangerous?

It's very dangerous if you lose control of your airplane. General aviation statistics tell us that the most dangerous loss of control (LOC) accidents involved stalls and spins, often at low levels, and not successfully recovered by those hapless pilots who must have felt bewildered and horrified during their last few seconds in the air. Still, the FAA does not require spin training for private or commercial pilot certification. Perhaps the answer to that mystery is because an airplane must stall before it can spin, so teaching stall avoidance and recover should take care of the problem. But it hasn't. One reason is that under the right conditions an airplane can go from an imminent stall to a full spin in the click of a mic button. You'll read about those conditions later in the section on upset recoveries.

Flight instructor candidates are required to demonstrate recovery from a spin, but often with less than one turn. Not even fully developed. Just a quick scare and it's over in a heartbeat. That kind of a spin introduction certainly does not prepare or encourage CFIs to teach spin recoveries to their student pilots. But I think they should—and here's how I think it should be done.

For starters, I believe pilots would benefit from learning how to recover from accelerated stalls and spins, and then recover from simulated climb-out and landing stalls and spins, all of this, of course, at a safe altitude with spin-competent aircraft and with a spin-savvy certified flight instructor. This training would not take much flying time, and would help prepare pilots to maintain control of their airplane in some of the most common, yet precarious, circumstances. I also recommend basic aerobatic training, and there's an important reason for this.

Sharpen your flight senses

Basic aerobatic and upset recovery skills can sharpen a pilot's vigilance for factors that could trigger an upset. I've witnessed first-hand how the flight training described in this book can sensitize a pilot's feel for a skid or slip (possible precursors to a snap-spin), become more aware of flight-control responsiveness (high angle of attack = mushy control response), even becoming attuned to the changing wind sound when airspeed changes. Those sensory skills give you greater spatial orientation and situational awareness, which helps you fly more mindfully and safely.

As a bonus, learning to better control your airplane could be the most exciting and rewarding aviation experience you've ever had.

All of the above is why I wrote this book.

The value of errors

I think I've witnessed every kind of student error you can imagine. Errors that occur during aerobatic and upset flight training can provide valuable teaching moments because they give students a chance to learn from them. This book explains common errors, detection methods, preventions, and remedies.

A bit about my experience

For over 50 years as an aerobatic instructor, I've been privileged to teach aerobatics and upset recoveries to pilots of many backgrounds, from low-time pilots who want more flying confidence in general, to professional pilots who want to bring bird-like freedom and stick-and-rudder excitement back into their flying. I speak to both of those orientations in this book. In addition to my Certified Flight Instructor (CFI) rating, I hold a Certified Distance Education Instructor (CDEI) designation, and I put both of those instructional skills to work when I designed the curricula and lesson plans you will soon learn about.

Are You a Little Nervous About Flying Weird Attitudes?

Don't worry—you've been through this before...

When you first learned to fly an airplane, making precise turns, climbs, and glides, it likely felt challenging, maybe a little scary—perhaps even risky. But it only felt that way at first, right? You soon became fluent with controlling the airplane, and normal flight operations became increasingly intuitive. Likewise, when stretching your limits with basic aerobatics, spins, and upset recoveries, it might at first seem a little edgy. You'll soon roll and loop and spin as if the airplane is an extension of your mind and body. I've never talked to a bird about this, but it must be the way they feel when they twirl and soar through the sky with abandon.

Here's how you fly with more fun

Psychological research has shown that the way you mentally frame an experience will directly affect how you react to it. If you think of something as fun, it will be. If you think of it as scary, it will be. For example, when each of my three non-pilot daughters reached 12 years old, I let them perform a loop all by themselves (with me monitoring the controls from the back seat). I introduced this experience by asking, "Do you want to have a lot of fun doing an easy loop?" By saying "yes," they framed the experience, and each of them giggled all the way through the maneuver. (By the way, my instruction was simply "Pull the stick all the way back and when we're right-side up again, put the stick back where it was." To this day, the only flying skill each of them has is flying an egg-shaped loop.) The point of all this is that if you think about your aerobatic and upset exercises as fun, you'll be smiling all the way through them. If you ever feel anxious before a maneuver, simply tell yourself that you are *excited*—same emotion, different connotation, very different experience.

But are you qualified to learn basic life-saving maneuvers?

I can't tell you specifically how many prior flying hours are necessary to learn basic aerobatic and upset recovery skills. But if you are a private pilot, you had to learn the basic flying skills needed to learn the entire syllabus of maneuvers in this book. In fact, before the 1950s, flight instructors routinely taught their students to recover from spins before letting them fly solo.

Simply put, you are probably ready for aerobatic and upset training if you want to fly competently beyond your current set of abilities and limitations. For example:

- If you get anxious when you feel the ripple of a stall, or if you've never practiced recovering from spins, then you could gain more confidence and spin awareness from learning spin and advanced stall recoveries.
- If you've ever watched an airshow and marveled at how much fun the show pilots must be having, then it might be time for you to experience that excitement (but at a safer altitude!).
- If your flying in general—personal or professional—has become less exciting, more routine, and less frequent, then learning to fly the maneuvers in this book can help you revive the enthusiasm that originally attracted you to aviation, along with reviving your pure joy of flight.

Loop and roll to keep control

I came up with this book title because looping and rolling are the basic ingredients for virtually all other aerobatic maneuvers, except for spin maneuvers. You'll also learn spin recoveries in this curriculum because an unintended stall or spin can happen by exceeding the critical angle of attack in any attitude, including aerobatics and during normal operation maneuvers. As pilots have done since the dawn of aviation, you'll begin by learning basic skills, then use those skills to learn more complex skills, and then progressing to some of the most advanced aerobatic skills. You'll then learn how those skills can help you regain control in loss of control (LOC) incidents, commonly known as upsets.

How This Book is Organized

The job of a syllabus is to outline the topics covered during a course of study, the curriculum's job is to provide the actual material taught—both in this book and during flight instruction by a competent aerobatic certified flight instructor. The curriculum you will be reading covers the knowledge about skills and competencies you will be learning during your flight instruction. The fundamental difference between a syllabus and curriculum, therefore, is that the former is like a table of contents, and the latter is the body of knowledge and skills to be learned.

Here's a closer look:

1. **Syllabus** – The list of maneuvers and topics covered in this book's curriculum. The syllabus lists the knowledge and practical categories of the training program, both on the ground and practiced in the air with a competent aerobatic flight instructor.

2. **Curriculum** – The actual content and instructions of the course, such as the action steps to perform maneuvers, learning how to correct and prevent errors, and how to safely abort maneuvers when errors become uncorrectable. Upset recovery techniques are also covered.

3. **Lesson Plans** – Each lesson plan within the curriculum lists the learning objectives, and gives a step-by-step explanation of control inputs and spatial orientation references. Each lesson also recommends ways to determine correctness and precision.

4. **Instructor tips** – I enjoy exchanging aerobatic instruction tips with other instructors, but since a two-way conversation isn't possible with a book, I'll sprinkle a few of my instructional methods where they seem relevant, meant for both instructors and learner with the hope my thoughts will enhance the instructor-learner collaboration.

The building block syllabus design

The aerobatic and upset curricula of this book is based on a building block method that matches how adults learn best—using something you know to learn something new. The collection of knowledge you'll learn from this book, plus the skills you learn in the air with a flight instructor, will gradually accumulate to help you learn increasingly complex skills.

Big value from a little homework

If you use this book to brief and debrief yourself before and after each flight training mission, you'll get much more value from your instruction time in the air. That will save you time, frustration, and money. Reading each lesson plan prior to coming to the airport will also help you approach your training flight with foresight, enthusiasm and confidence.

Solo practice warning

Do not attempt any aerobatic maneuver the first time without your qualified aerobatic CFI in the cockpit with you, and do not perform aerobatic maneuvers solo unless your instructor advises you that you are competent to perform the maneuver safely. You must be able to identify and correct errors, and be able to safely recover if you have to abort the maneuver.

When you are ready to practice a maneuver solo, this book can also help you refine your maneuver skills. Whenever you cannot figure something out, however, ask your instructor for suggestions. If that doesn't help, schedule a training flight.

Don't shortcut your learning

You'll be doing yourself an injustice if you stop your flight training after learning just a few basic aerobatic maneuvers. You might be able to fly a handful of maneuvers well enough to impress your friends, but you'll be glad you had upset recovery training—and know how to abort maneuvers—if something goes wrong.

Each lesson plan is fully explained

Each flight lesson in this curriculum will contain these elements:

1. A bit of history about how and when some of the maneuvers were first performed.
2. A pre-flight briefing to help you understand the maneuver and optimize your flight time.
3. A step-by-step explanation of how to perform each maneuver.
4. Suggested ground references to help you maintain spatial orientation and precision during each maneuver.
5. Common maneuver errors with suggested remedies.

Time Out to Share Thoughts with Fellow Flight Instructors

Even though I insert some ideas for other flight instructors, based on my own experiences, I don't mean to imply that I know more about aerobatics or instructing than they do. In fact, I have learned a lot over the years from other instructors by exchanging training ideas with them, sometimes traveling to receive advanced aerobatic instructor training from aerobatic CFIs in other states. Although I do not compete in aerobatic contests, I have attended International Aerobatic Club judging classes to help my competitive students win at aerobatic contests.

A handy training guidebook

The curriculum and lesson plans in this book have evolved over five decades of aerobatic flight instructing. If you are an aerobatic instructor who likes the way it progresses, perhaps your students will use it as a study guide, even if your training syllabus is presented in a different order. I've found that when students arrive at the airport with some knowledge about that day's flight lesson, they are prepared to convert that knowledge into a new skill set. That preparation can give students the ideal learning attitudes: low anxiety, moderate excitement, high enthusiasm.

The curriculum in this book contains detailed sequential lesson plans, but—depending on the flying experience, learning rate, and temperament of your student—you might proceed slower or faster than the sample lessons. I start each training flight lesson with a short review of maneuvers learned in a previous lesson, making sure students can fly them to both the right and the left. I might hook two together, like a loop followed by a roll. If a student found a past maneuver difficult, I might revisit that one—unless the student felt physically uncomfortable from flying it. Dutch rolls come to mind as a typical vertigo maker. It's a great maneuver before each lesson to get rudder and aileron inputs coordinated, but not if it unsettles the student. Too many rolling maneuvers or spins can bring on a bit of vertigo, more so than high G maneuvers. I often ask my student if they'd like to practice a prior maneuver again, giving them a chance to feel more comfortable and confident with it.

If you are CFI thinking about teaching aerobatics...

... perhaps this book will help you get started. The aviation world needs more CFIs to help pilots learn how to keep control of their airplanes in extreme attitudes, and to anticipate and recover safely from upsets. Basic aerobatic and advanced upset training can give pilots a greater mastery of their airplane and more flying fun than they ever thought possible. A basic aerobatic and upset course that follows the syllabus of this book will take only 12 to 15 flight hours. I also show two abbreviated courses, one for about 5 hours and one for about 3 hours. I think teaching aerobatics is more exciting than certification training, and you'll be helping pilots avoid or recover from losing control of their airplanes.

Part 1
Pre-flight Briefing

Tale Spins   *By Arland Nau*

"I feel like I'm forgetting something."

Chapter 1
How Aerobatic Skills Benefits All Your Flying

Fly More Precisely and Mindfully

As an added benefit of aerobatic training, it will help you become more precise with all your flying. You'll learn to maneuver more mindfully, making even the steepest turn coordinated, properly applying the right control inputs for a perfect maneuver, and being mindful of your airspeed and angle of attack.

Flying with finesse

If you watch videos of aerobatics, you'll see jazzy fast-paced routines. There's nothing wrong with putting on a show if done safely, but for now, try to think of aerobatics as more of a Straus waltz than rock and roll. Think precision. Think grace and elegance. Granted, airshow pilots must thrill the crowd with low-level buzz jobs, but don't approach learning the art of aerobatic flying with those models. Birds don't fly that way, and neither should you.

Be kind to your passengers

When your aerobatic CFI says you are competent enough to fly specific maneuvers solo, resist the temptation to immediately take your friends up for a wild ride. You need to practice solo for a while without distractions or hubris. And when you do introduce your passengers to aerobatics, give them an exciting (versus terrorizing) ride that will let them feel safe. Limit vertigo-producing turning maneuvers. As they say in show business, always end with them wanting more.

But they won't want more if you make them dizzy or sick. Instead, let them experience a perfectly coordinated aileron roll or barrel roll, for example, they'll remember that low-G experience and brag about it for the rest of their lives. Anything more for a non-pilot will likely be a frightening blur.

Spin Recovery Skills Make All Your Flying Safer

A place for spin training

According to accident statistics in a recent Joseph T. Nall Report, unintended stalls and spins, especially during low level operations, are still the top causes of general aviation accidents and fatalities, right behind flying into bad weather. It's always better to avoid an unintended spin than to recover from one, especially when a low altitude might make a recovery impossible. That's why I believe that all pilots should at least learn to recover from accelerated stalls and spins, practiced at a safe altitude. That training can help you become more sensitive to how the controls feel when approaching a critical angle of attack. It can also help you feel slips and skids with your body movements, especially when you might be distracted while watching for traffic and ground references.

Pinched maneuvers

Later in this book, you'll read about how other maneuvers, when pinched (i.e., pulling the stick back excessively during a high angle of attack), can put you into a stall and spin, sometimes immediately, even while diving. An example would be the backside of a too-tight loop, when the airplane's nose is pointing straight down. That, sadly, has happened to airshow pilots who didn't allow enough altitude to recover. You'll experience how airplanes can stall above their published stall speed if the stick is pulled back too vigorously. A snap roll, for example, is initiated at airspeeds well above V_s (stall speed), and while in a horizontal straight-and-level flight configuration.

The ingredients of a spin

While we're on the subject of spins, a wing must stall before the airplane can spin (although the sequence can seem instantaneous), or both wings must stall with one stalled more deeply than the other one. What's more, if you hold an airplane into a stall by holding back on the stick (something, sadly, non-aerobatic pilots will often instinctively do in a panic), then it will require fast footwork on the rudders to avoid spinning. You'll learn that rudder dance in one of this curriculum's lesson plans.

Although stalling is not directly related to speed or attitude, it *is* directly related to angle of attack. When the degree of that angle approaches the high teens (on most airplane wings), the airflow is disrupted enough to rob the wing of lift.

Sensing spins before they start

Besides learning to have fun with various stall/spin recoveries (and yes, they *are* fun when you begin to feel in control), your senses will become alert for inadvertent impending stalls. You'll sometimes feel an imminent stall in your mushy-feeling control responses, hear it in reduced wind noise, feel air starting to burble over the wing—all of this perhaps before the stall warning starts to beep.

Extreme attitudes

Although this book will cover an assortment of stall and spin maneuvers, it will also cover non-stalled extreme attitude upsets, such as an unintended inverted dive. An inverted dive can happen when the airplane rolls past a 90° bank. Without training, many pilots are prone to instinctively pull back on the stick, which forces them to recover with a half loop, also known as a split-S. But unless started at a low airspeed, a split-S will quickly dive through valuable altitude, maybe exceeding the airplane's airspeed limits, perhaps overstress airframe and the pilot with heavy G-forces during the pullout. Instead of a dangerous recovery like that, you you'll learn to push on the stick to maintain altitude, while rolling upright. Quick, safe, and relatively uneventful.

Fly More Confidently

Pushing past your limitations

Many aerobatic students have told me that their aerobatic and upset recovery training has made them feel more relaxed and confident in all types of flying, even during simple cross-country flights. That confidence is the reward you'll earn when you safely push past your prior aeronautical limits.

It reminds me of when I was a young boy scout learning how to paddle a canoe at scout camp. Compared to my dad's wide, stable fishing boat, the canoe seemed tippy and finicky, threatening to capsize with the slightest wiggle. When I enrolled in advanced training for the canoeing merit badge, I learned canoe techniques to handle all kinds of conditions. The most fun exercise was paddling several feet from shore with a buddy, both of us in swim suits, and purposely swamping the canoe. I was surprised by how the canoe easily banked to one side, but it resisted going past the gunnel in spite of us leaning and rocking to spill it over. Eventually we swamped the canoe but it stayed afloat while we wiggled back in and started bailing water with our hands. After that experience, my confidence in canoes spiked, and remains so to this day when I canoe in Minnesota's beautiful lakes and rivers.

That canoe learning experience flashed back when I started learning the maneuvering limits of an airplane during my initial aerobatic training. I soon felt more confident about aborting maneuvers or recovering after mishaps. I was able to mentally stay further ahead of every airplane I flew, sensing any lack of coordination in a turn, even before the inclinometer's sluggish ball could ooze to one side or the other.* I felt the subtle lack of control authority in my fingers when airspeed was low and the wing was on the edge of the critical angle of attack. As my confidence reached new levels, every aspect of flying became more relaxed and fun, and I was more mindful of my airplane's performance.

It also made corrections and recoveries decisive and expedient. As an example, I'll return to one of the two times that I was rolled inverted at low altitude.

It happened in Alaska when I was earning my floatplane rating, and also learning mountain flying techniques. During one training flight in a Super Cub on floats, my instructor and I flew up a canyon to practice box canyon turn-arounds. As we entered the canyon, a sudden downdraft from the lee of the closest mountain rolled us past knife edge, and I immediately, reflexively, pushed on the stick to prevent an inverted dive, while rolling the wings level with full aileron and hard rudder. There was no altitude loss, and I continued flying merrily along. After a few moments of silence, my instructor said "Okay, turn around. We're going back." When I asked him why, he said "That really freaked me out." He said he'd never rolled that steeply before, and he wanted to get out of the airplane for a while to collect himself. Sure, it took me by surprise, too, but otherwise it was no big deal to me. The experience was important to me, however, because it made me realize how aerobatic training would have made that CFI smile instead of "freaking out" over an incident that was corrected well within safety margins. It also made me realize that without my aerobatic training, we might not have survived the upset.

---

* (The inclinometer is the "ball" part of the multi-purpose "turn and bank indicator," also known as the "turn coordinator," or the "turn and slip" indicator. The "two-minute" turn and bank portion is driven by an electric gyro, and the ball is suspended in a fluid-filled, arc-shaped glass tube. It looks like a smile. As you know, when your turns are coordinated, no matter how steep the bank, the ball will be in the middle of the arc. Some aerobatic airplanes also have an upside-down inclinometer for inverted flight. It looks like a frown.)

A final word about confidence

Early in my aerobatic instructing career, I spent a few days in Venice, Florida, getting advanced spin and aerobatic training from Bill Thomas, the nationally-known aerobatic champion and instructor. After he finished entering my last flight with him in my log book, he handed it back to me and said, "My parting advice is to be careful. And when you get really good, be *very* careful."

I'd add that when you are very careful, you'll have even more fun.

Chapter 2
How to Make Extreme Flying Fun

Tips for feeling relaxed, mindful, and comfortable.

Taming Pesky Physiological Signals

When you first start learning aerobatics and upset recoveries, you'll likely feel a bit uncomfortable at times. That's because any new learning situation (remember when you first learned to drive?) can create some anxiety. That mild stress can initially make hard pullups and steep banks seem alarming. That's because your physiological warning system will signal you that "Hey, something's weird," which is meant to arouse you to fix the situation. Your brain is pre-wired to deliver those warning messages to protect you. For instance, if you are falling, you'll automatically look for something to grab or someplace safe to fall.

Similarly, overcoming G-forces might seem like a struggle at first. If a person's arm weighs, say, 10 pounds, it would weigh 40 pounds during a brief 4-G pullup, as in a loop entry. You might be distracted at first by the heavy feeling. Your brain, however, will eventually extinguish the anxious discomfort, because an unheeded feeling will eventually be deemed unneeded. Similarly, flying inverted the first time could make you feel like you have to use lots of heavy forward stick pressure to keep the nose "up" (toward your feet). But with a little practice, you'll soon realize that flying straight and level while inverted requires very little muscle power to keep the stick forward. By the way, I enjoy the sensation of being inverted. It's like when I was a kid hanging upside down from playground equipment or tree branches.

Another experience you might have at first is not fully seeing what the airplane is actually doing during an aerobatic maneuver. You might be looking ahead at blank blue sky, or it might be happening so fast that it looks like a blur. But things appear to slow down with even a little practice. They don't really slow down, of course, but your perceptions will speed up, making your experience seem slower. When that happens, you will not feel Gs or rolls so much, and your increased spatial orientation will help you keep track of your position. In time, extreme attitudes will become more of a visual experience than a sensory distraction.

All of these physiological reactions are normal, but if they distract you too much, tell your instructor you'd like to take a straight-and-level break for a while, or that you'd like to return to the airport. There's nothing wrong with easing into this new type of flying.

Concentration Overload

If your concentration starts to feel strained, take a timeout until you regain your mental sharpness. If you continue to feel mentally taxed, it's time to sight-see and relax for a few minutes, or perhaps even return to the airport. You can make that decision at any time, or your instructor might make it for you. A good aerobatic instructor will want to know how you are doing, and if it's not so good, he or she will call the training mission a success and adjourn the lesson. From a learning theory standpoint, when your cognitive resources are tapped out, your learning curve flattens. In other words, you are more preoccupied with your discomfort than with your performance. Even worse, you might end the lesson feeling discouraged. I can assure you that no instructor wants that to happen, not only because of compassion for you as a student, but to curtail any thoughts about giving up. So, don't worry about making the training flight too short. Many world-class aerobatic competitors and airshow pilots limit their practice routines to around 20 minutes. Quality is always more important than quantity when it comes to the demands of learning a new way to fly.

Handling G-Loads

During normal flight operations, you are pulling 1 G, which is one times your weight on the ground. You are pulling one G right now while reading this book. When flying straight and level while inverted, you are pulling 1 negative G, or -1 G. You might also feel a negative G, or perhaps zero Gs, if you aggressively pitch the nose forward. (The curriculum in this book does not include "outside" maneuvers that require this.) When you fly a 45° upline and then suddenly push the stick forward, you'll feel light in the seat, less than one G, maybe even weightlessness if you pushed hard enough. If you do become weightless, anything loose in the cockpit might float around. For that reason, make sure you leave things like loose change and combs at the airport, and make sure charts and other papers are securely stowed or clipped to something in the cockpit.

To better handle heavy G-load maneuvers, simply tighten your stomach muscles during G-forces—but like with any physical exercise, remember to continue breathing. By the way, there are fewer heavy G-load maneuvers than you might think. You'll feel heavy at the start and end of looping maneuvers, but not at all during most rolling maneuvers. Whenever you've banked an airplane 60 degrees in a coordinated turn, you were pulling two Gs. If you stand on your kitchen chair and jump off, you'll probably pull 6 or so instantaneous Gs when your feet hit the floor. Loops pull about 4 Gs, but only for a few seconds during the beginning and ending.

Minding Mind and Body

Your pre-flight health

Get a good night's sleep and limit alcohol consumption the night before. Avoid coming to the airport for your aerobatic flight lesson with a full stomach, or with an empty stomach. Avoid acidic drinks like coffee or lemonade, and fizzy drinks like sodas. Feeling comfortable is the key. Some people find eating a piece of ginger candy before a flight is gastronomically soothing.

Maintain Mindfulness

A good way to prepare for an aerobatic flight (or any flight, for that matter) is to sit in your car a minute or two when you arrive at the airport, and simply concentrate on your breathing. Closing your eyes will help avoid distractions. This simple mindfulness technique will center and calm you, and you'll perform better with more enjoyment. Feeling overly excited and anxious, on the other hand, can distract you and interfere with your learning and fun. Another wise tip from aerobatic champion Bill Thomas is, "God invented time so everything wouldn't happen at once." In other words, be mindful of each moment, one at a time, before and during any flight.

The thrills will mellow

My first aerobatic maneuver was when my primary CFI took me through a simple loop. I held my breath through most of it. I had never moved through airspace so radically, so quickly, flying upside down, pulling Gs—in short, it was a thrill. After getting my commercial certificate, I completed an aerobatic course, but the thrills gradually mellowed into the pure, exciting joy of flight, moving with precision through any attitude. When I see birds playing in the air, I stop and watch. I know how much fun they're having.

Sharing Thoughts with Aerobatic Flight Instructors

(If you're a student it's okay to listen in.)

Self-study and preparation

My motivation for writing this manual is to help students prepare for their aerobatic training flights, and then review them when they return home. As you know, students learn more in the air when they've invested some study time on the ground.

The power of suggestion

Each of my aerobatic students over the years have taught me something about how to better manage their learning experiences. For example, I found that if I ask a student "How do you feel?" he might not have been feeling anything until I brought up the subject. My question might have been suggestive, perhaps triggering unsettling feelings. Instead of asking that question, I ask "How are you doing?" They know what I mean, and they don't have to tap into their feelings to answer me.

Time to return to the airfield

I get more information about how students are doing by watching. I look for lapses of attention and slowing responses. When those conditions appear, the learning curve is going flat. If there's no more learning taking place, the student is being put through a negative experience. That's when I declare the training mission a success (it always is, no matter how long the lesson, or how much has been learned during that time), and then we head back to the airfield.

Vertigo

I assure my aerobatic students that heightened feelings are common for all pilots new to aerobatic maneuvers, and I reassure them that their body and mind will extinguish those reactions over time, usually a short time. Until then, I limit turning maneuvers. For physiological reasons I will cover later in this book, too much turning is the top vertigo producer. The symptoms of vertigo, as you know, range from momentary confusion to upset stomachs.

Learning rates

I slow the training down or speed it up according to the student's ideal learning pace. For example, it can't be too fast-paced for most ex-fighter pilots, or too precise for most professional pilots. But no matter what their background is, I make sure their cognitive resources and neurological systems have a chance to keep up with the new sensations they are experiencing and the spatial orientation challenges they are solving. If in doubt, I check their ongoing internal experience with "How are you doing?" (Once in a while a cocky student will reply with "Fine, how are you doing?" My standard reply is "I'm scared out of my wits.")

We have the easy job

As an instructor, I have to remember that I'm not so much "teaching" aerobatics and upset recoveries as I am helping pilots learn. They have the hard job, and I need to be patient while they practice what I'm instructing, and have fun during the process.

Fixing errors

When a student is having trouble with a particular maneuver, we'll discuss possible reasons. I'll know the answer, but I want her to learn how to accurately self-evaluate. A critical part of aerobatic and upset recovery training is learning how to identify what went wrong, and knowing how to fix it next time. After a brief evaluation, I'll give the student a practice exercise that might remedy the problem. For example, if a student has trouble exiting an aileron roll at his entry heading, I might tell him to try using even more rudder than he thinks is necessary. If the student "discovers" the remedy this way, it will be added permanently to his skill set. If the problem is not fully understanding what the maneuver is supposed to look like and feel like, I might demonstrate the maneuver while the student follows with his hands and feet lightly on the controls. If the problem is spatial disorientation, I might tell the student to glance at the airplane's nose or wingtips relative to a visual reference on the ground while I fly the maneuver.

I've also found that it can be valuable to demonstrate a maneuver again after the student has practiced it once or twice. That allows the student compare his control inputs and vision of the maneuver with mine. I might fly an erroneous version of a maneuver first, and then follow with a correct version.

20

Productive feedback

I never tell a student her performance of a maneuver was "good" or "bad." Feedback is important, but if the student becomes preoccupied with my judgements and approvals, it could distract her from fully concentrating on the maneuver. I point out flubs with something like, "Did you notice that the nose seemed to dish out at the end of the roll?" Not "good," or not "bad," just objective feedback instead of judgmental feedback. If the student gets stuck, I'll give a concrete suggestion like "Try it with more rudder this time."

Ground debriefing

While flying back to the airport after a lesson, I usually list all the things the student just learned, and assure him that the lesson's goals had been met. I save any critiques until we get back to the hangar. This gives the student time to unwind, clear her head, and concentrate on the pattern, landing, and taxiing.

Progress happens

Every lesson, no matter what happens is a learning experience—and that's progress. Your student can learn more from botching a maneuver a few times than he can from doing it perfectly the first time. If a student repeatedly struggles with a difficult maneuver, I assure her each flub is bringing her closer to mastery.

A preview for next time

Sometimes if the student is still feeling fresh at the end of a flight lesson, I'll demo a maneuver that we'll be covering in the next lesson. But I never cast a shadow on the student's newly acquired skills by showing off with some wild sequence of complex maneuvers. That could easily undo any feelings of success and progress the student acquired during the training flight. What we are capable of doesn't matter to students, and they aren't paying us for a joy ride. What *does* matter is the satisfaction they get from learning to stretch their personal limits and to become better pilots.

Chapter 3
FARs Regulating Aerobatic Activities

I'm showing Federal Aviation Regulations (FARs) pertinent to aerobatic flight, current as of January, 2020. I'm not an attorney, so I can't interpret them for you, but the language seems straightforward to me. I have indented the lists for easier reading. Notice that each FAR describes aerobatic flight differently. Also note when parachutes are required, and that you need to check their currency.

FAR §91.303   Aerobatic flight.

No person may operate an aircraft in aerobatic flight—

(a) Over any congested area of a city, town, or settlement;

(b) Over an open air assembly of persons;

(c) Within the lateral boundaries of the surface areas of Class B, Class C, Class D, or Class E airspace designated for an airport;

(d) Within 4 nautical miles of the center line of any Federal airway;

(e) Below an altitude of 1,500 feet above the surface; or

(f) When flight visibility is less than 3 statute miles.

For the purposes of this section, aerobatic flight means an intentional maneuver involving an abrupt change in an aircraft's attitude, an abnormal attitude, or abnormal acceleration, not necessary for normal flight.

[Doc. No. 18834, 54 FR 34308, Aug. 18, 1989, as amended by Amdt. 91-227, 56 FR 65661, Dec. 17, 1991]

FAR §91.307 Parachutes and parachuting.

(a) No pilot of a civil aircraft may allow a parachute that is available for emergency use to be carried in that aircraft unless it is an approved type and has been packed by a certificated and appropriately rated parachute rigger—

    (1) Within the preceding 180 days, if its canopy, shrouds, and harness are composed exclusively of nylon, rayon, or other similar synthetic fiber or materials that are substantially resistant to damage from mold, mildew, or other fungi and other rotting agents propagated in a moist environment; or

    (2) Within the preceding 60 days, if any part of the parachute is composed of silk, pongee, or other natural fiber or materials not specified in paragraph (a)(1) of this section.

(b) Except in an emergency, no pilot in command may allow, and no person may conduct, a parachute operation from an aircraft within the United States except in accordance with part 105 of this chapter.

(c) Unless each occupant of the aircraft is wearing an approved parachute, no pilot of a civil aircraft carrying any person (other than a crewmember) may execute any intentional maneuver that exceeds—

    (1) A bank of 60 degrees relative to the horizon; or

    (2) A nose-up or nose-down attitude of 30 degrees relative to the horizon.

(d) Paragraph (c) of this section does not apply to—

    (1) Flight tests for pilot certification or rating; or

    (2) Spins and other flight maneuvers required by the regulations for any certificate or rating when given by—

        (i) A certificated flight instructor; or
        (ii) An airline transport pilot instructing in accordance with §61.67 of this chapter.

(e) For the purposes of this section, approved parachute means—

    (1) A parachute manufactured under a type certificate or a technical standard order (C-23 series); or

    (2) A personnel-carrying military parachute identified by an NAF, AAF, or AN drawing number, an AAF order number, or any other military designation or specification number.

[Doc. No. 18334, 54 FR 34308, Aug. 18, 1989, as amended by Amdt. 91-255, 62 FR 68137,

Dec. 30, 1997; Amdt. 91-268, 66 FR 23553, May 9, 2001; Amdt. 91-305, 73 FR 69530, Nov. 19, 2008]

Chapter 4
Before Starting Your Engine

Aerobatic airplanes have some design and safety features that might be new to you. Here are a few common ones.

Aerobatic Aircraft Design Basics

Aircraft limitations

You should fly aerobatics only in an aircraft designed for this purpose, and limit your maneuvers to those approved by the manufacturer. Consult the aircraft's pilot operating handbook (POH) for maneuvers which are approved, and note their recommended entry speeds. Also take note of their positive and negative G-loads limitations, which are typically at least 6 Gs positive and 4 negative.

Wing Camber

Normal category airplanes generally have wings that are arced on the top and flatter on the bottom. But the top and bottom surface camber of aerobatic airplane wings are sometimes completely, or somewhat more, symmetrical, which creates better lift during inverted flight. Take notice of the wing shape when you pre-flight your aerobatic airplane. If the bottom is slightly convex, that's what I'm talking about. That aerobatic wing design compromises a little right-side up lift, so when you reduce the power to idle, you'll notice a steeper descent than with a normal category airplane. That will become most evident during your final approach to a landing.

Dihedral

Dihedral is the upward angle of a wing from its root to its tip. This gives stability during normal flight, but too much dihedral can make inverted flight noticeably less stable. For that reason, there is sometimes less dihedral in aerobatic category airplane wings.

Biplane roll rates

The two short wings of a biplane will give a faster roll rate than with a monoplane, all other design factors being the same. To illustrate that shortened-length effect, you might have noticed that figure skaters pull their arms in to increase their spinning speed, and then let their arms out to slow down for their next maneuver. Aerobatic biplanes typically have ailerons on both top and bottom wings—four ailerons in all—which also revs up the roll rate.

Aileron assists

Some aerobatic airplanes have a fixed "spade" or "shovel" extending from the ailerons to assist your stick inputs, acting like a trim surface to reduce the amount of muscle power needed to quickly move the stick right or left. Although spades lighten the needed stick pressure, the rudders will still feel heavy. I warn new aerobatic students about this disparity so they don't think they are using too much rudder in rolling maneuvers. One pound of pressure on the stick might need, say, 2 pounds of pressure on the rudder to counter adverse yaw. (That's an illustrative measure, not a scientific one.)

Inverted fuel systems

Aerobatic airplanes sometimes have inverted fuel systems to support sustained inverted flight. On the Super Decathlon, for example, there's a small fuel tank under and forward of the instrument panel, which feeds fuel to the engine by gravity while upside down. It takes a few minutes of right-side up flying for gravity to refill this little tank from the wing tanks. Check the aircraft's POH for information about the aircraft's fuel system, paying attention to how much sustainable inverted flight time is available, and how many minutes of right-side up flying it will take for the inverted tank to refill itself. If your aerobatic airplane does not have an inverted fuel system, you will have to avoid prolonged inverted flight, otherwise the engine will stop. I probably don't need to tell you this, but if the engine quits while inverted, roll right-side up and restart the engine.

Inverted oil systems

While inverted, many aerobatic airplane engines also have a complex oil distribution system that will maintain lubrication throughout the inside of the engine while inverted. Lycoming, for example, has a system of oil tubes outside the engine block to redistribute oil while inverted.

Throttle management

If your aerobatic airplane does not have a constant- speed propeller, you'll be learning power management from your instructor during some maneuvers. For example, you'll be adding power—probably full power—on the pullup during a loop. When you are diving down through the backside of the loop, you'll reduce power, probably to idle, to manage your airspeed. Consult your POH and discuss the procedure for your aircraft with your aerobatic flight instructor.

Airplane design drag

Aerobatic airplanes are sometimes "draggy." They are designed to be nimble, not necessarily streamlined for fast cross-country flying. Drag helps reduce the amount of speed you gain and the amount of altitude you lose during a maneuver's downline (i.e., when diving). It also helps you perform a series of aerobatic maneuvers within a relatively small box of airspace.

Visibility

Outside visibility is often increased in aerobatic airplanes so the pilot can look "up" while inverted to see ground reference points or air traffic below. This is provided by dome (or "greenhouse") canopies, or windows in the roof. The enhanced visibility also helps during clearing turns, when you have to look up, down, and all around. During looping maneuvers, for example, you need to see traffic above and below you, whether you are inverted or not, and you need to see ground references regardless of your attitude.

Other aerobatic design features

Other typical features of aerobatic airplanes include things like quick release doors or canopies for emergency bailout, removable seat or back cushions to accommodate parachutes, wide seatbelts for comfort while inverted. There also may be an additional seatbelt for extra safety, and beefed up shoulder harnesses, all of which are attached at one or two points for quick release. Throttles are usually reachable without having to extend your G-force-heavy arm during high G pullups.

Gyroscopic instruments

Attitude indicators with gyros are often absent or can be caged (locked) during aerobatic flight. The extreme attitude changes during aerobatics will tumble gyros, making them dizzily useless until they have several minutes to right themselves. Besides, you should be looking out the windows to determine your attitude, not at an interpretive instrument.

Landing gears

Aerobatic airplanes often have a conventional landing gear (i.e., "tail draggers") instead of a nosewheel. Besides the extra weight and drag of a nosewheel, the only reason I can think of for the popularity of tail draggers is that they look more traditional and nostalgic, harkening back to the days of daredevils, barnstormers and WWII fighter pilots. I'm not saying that design trappings are unimportant, though. An aerobatic airplane should look cool, with dazzling starburst paint job and all. If you have special flying skills, you should fly a special looking airplane, one that makes you stand out.

Pre-flight Inspections

Always perform a thorough pre-flight inspection before flying any airplane, but pay particular attention to an aerobatic airplane's vulnerabilities and special features. Aerobatic airplanes undergo higher G-loads and erratic maneuvers, so give careful attention to the aircraft's stress points.

For instance, look for things that could restrict or interfere with control functions, such as loose seat restraints, and missing or defective seat blocks. Inspect for loose objects that might have ended up in the tail, especially with taildraggers. Over the years of tapping against the aft bottoms of Pitts Special and Super Decathlon tails, I've found coins, clipped zip ties, and a plastic comb, any of which could lock up a control cable pulley. If something sounds loose when you tap underneath the lowest point in the tail, remove the nearest inspection plate and feel around for the culprit. While on the topic of housekeeping, you should vacuum the carpet or floorboards once in a while. This will prevent a sand shower when your roll from inverted to upright.

Look for wrinkles, especially along the tail, at the wing root, and along the wings, paying special attention for signs that could indicate something bent, cracked, or broken. Use a flashlight to inspect engine mounts and exposed control cable attachments. These are just generalized suggestions, so read your airplane's POH and have your instructor coach you properly through your first pre-flight. You should also be shown how to check your parachutes for FAA-approved inspection currency and proper functioning. For example, I once found a bent rip cord pin, which would have made the parachute inoperable. (I later found out that a young lineman had pulled the parachute out of the airplane by the "handle," which was a ripcord, and it felt slack so he checked and found that one of the pins looked loose. He bent it to make sure it would stay in place.)

Bring along a leakproof motion discomfort bag, unless there's already one in the airplane (and there probably will be). It's nice to have a leakproof bag handy, more for psychological comfort than the chance it might be needed. You can buy commercial motion discomfort bags (or get them from accommodating airline flight crew members) and I use a big spring paper clip to fasten one on the door compartment or wherever else it can be reached by both parties. Secure other paper cargo such as charts and checklists with another clip. Anything loose in the cockpit will float around while inverted or weightless from a sudden pitch, and end up who knows where—maybe in the tail—so keep everything clipped in place.

This is by no means a comprehensive pre-flight checklist meant to cover all airplanes. Remember, consult your aircraft's POH and pay attention to the pre-flight inspection details emphasized by your flight instructor for the aircraft you'll be flying.

Practicing Emergency Egress

Egress procedures alert

The below egress practice suggestions are only examples intended as educational information, and might not apply to the egress system and parachute you use. Make sure you understand how the emergency door or canopy release works on the specific airplane you will be training in, and with the specific emergency parachute you will be wearing during training flights. Consult the airplane's POH for egress procedures, and the parachute manufacturer's instructions, along with guidance from your aerobatic flight instructor.

Don't worry, you won't practice emergency egress by actually bailing out. The best place to develop proper emergency procedures is on the ground. Practice the procedures the way martial arts students do, with deliberate, mindful, and unhurried actions to create mental imprints of each move during an emergency. If an emergency develops, the procedures will be already mentally in place. During my U.S. Army basic training, a drill instructor told us that in an emergency, we'd fall back on our training—whatever that training was. When things happen too fast to think about it, your behavior must be automatic.

To make sure your emergency egress training is effective, practice these three procedures while sitting in the aircraft.

1. **Release your headset and harness.** The harnesses in aerobatic airplanes should have a quick-release system, requiring one or two actions to get you completely freed from the seatbelts and shoulder straps. Practice this by sitting in the cockpit all strapped in with your headset on, and then remove your headset and free yourself with minimal inputs. Don't worry about speed at this point, just concentrate mindfully and deliberately while slowly going through the process.

2. **Release the egress door or canopy.** Unlike practicing harness and headset releasing, you don't need to actually release your airplane's egress system. After your flight instructor explains how the system works, mindfully touch each release ring and lever, or other release system. While touching each release in proper sequence, say aloud what you are touching and what the action should be (i.e., "Pull ring. Pull lever. Push door."). Do this slowly because you are imprinting the procedure in your mind.

3. **Bail out.** Your instructor will suggest the fastest, safest way to go from your seat to the wild blue yonder. It should include where to grab, where to step, how to leave the aircraft, and when and how to pull the rip cord. Watching skydiver videos might give you the impression that you'll float down through the sky before you open your chute, but actually, you'll fall like a rock until you pull your ripcord.

Unlike sport parachutes that use a sliding hoop to make the canopy open gradually and gently, safety parachutes are designed to pop open ASAP. When you're buckling up for your flight, make sure your parachute straps are comfortably snug to lessen the jolt when the canopy deploys.

During this ground practice, make sure that you can find the ripcord with your hand, but don't bail out with your hand on the ripcord because you might accidently yank the retaining pins free on the way out, which could get the canopy caught in or on the aircraft. Once you are free from the airplane—which will happen *very* fast—pull the ripcord all the way out. I repeat: *All the way out*, until it's dangling free in your hand. You want to make sure the release pins are not still holding the canopy in place.

(**NOTE:** Follow the manufacturer's instructions for the specific parachute you will be wearing.)

Most parachutes will allow you to turn, so that you can land facing into the wind (for the same reason you land airplanes into the wind). The ones I've seen have finger loops held in place by a 2-pound thread that you can pull free.

I suggest talking to—or better yet, visiting—your parachute's FAA-approved packer and consulting the manufacturer's manual for more information about the specific parachute you'll be wearing. I also suggest you consult parachute experts on how to land on the ground, in trees, and in water.

Part 2
Flight Training Syllabus

Tale Spins   *By Arland Nau*

"You loop and roll and twist and shout, then put your right foot in and shake it all about."

Introduction

The syllabus will be following a curriculum I have developed and refined throughout my 50+ years as an aerobatic certified flight instructor. It's based on a building-block approach to learning aerobatics, which means first learning fundamental maneuvers, then using those skills to learn more challenging maneuvers—and so on, gradually increasing your repertoire of skills.

The first lessons will expand your stick-and-rudder skills. You'll manage your airplane's energy to get optimum performance, and you'll increase your spatial awareness by flying through steep attitudes. From those basic piloting exercises, you'll learn the foundation skills of rolling, looping, and spin recovery, which are the three sturdy pillars that lead to many other fun maneuvers.

(Note: I use the term "Stick" throughout this book to mean the control stick or the control yoke.)

Let patience be your friend

My syllabus limits the number of rolling and turning maneuvers at first, because those are the potential vertigo inducers, and vertigo can temporarily mess with your overall sense of well-being. You are likely, however, to adapt to G-forces sooner than you might think. You will adapt even sooner to turns and G-forces if you practice the mindfulness exercise I mentioned earlier. If motion discomfort persists, ask your instructor to go easy at first. Some students have found comfort with wrist-worn devices that use either electronics or pressure points to curtail motion discomfort. Other students have found that chewable ginger candy sooths the GI system. The benefit of these might simply be placebo effect— but if it works, who cares?

I think the most reliable way to adapt to unusual movements and attitudes is to be patient. Don't be in a hurry to pack as many maneuvers as possible into the shortest possible time. Take it easy, pace yourself. Let your flight instructor know when you need a timeout break to sight-see for a few minutes (to center yourself, look at faraway objects, not directly down), and let your instructor know when you'd like to end a lesson. Your instructor will be glad that you are managing your experience, because then you are more likely to continue your training.

All this talk about discomfort aside, you are more likely to just feel excited and perfectly fine from your first flight and onward. I'm just trying to cover all the bases here.

Do your best for now, perfect it later

Although I recommend following the suggested sequence of maneuvers in this curriculum, that doesn't mean you need to perform a maneuver perfectly before learning the next one. As an example of my approach to flight training, once you can fly a loop that's somewhat round and you are aware of your errors, I'd let you tackle the next maneuver on the syllabus. The idea is to keep progressing at a comfortable pace, and let perfection come later during reviews and practices. This doesn't mean I would replace thoroughness with haste, but it does mean that at the beginning of the next lesson, I would let you make another loop, and you'd almost certainly make it rounder with fewer errors, even though you haven't practiced looping since the last lesson. It will seem like magic.

Mental magic

In addition to the practice-makes-perfect principle, your brain will continue learning even when you're not consciously thinking about it. That's why looping will seem easier next time. The maneuver will seem to slow down, giving you time to notice how the airplane is responding to your control inputs. You'll more carefully notice how it tracks your ground references. If you want to ramp up your mental learning power, reread the maneuver's steps and error corrections in this book, and take a couple of minutes each day in your easy chair to mentally fly the maneuver. Close your eyes and visualize the sky and ground. Imagine feeling the stick and rudders. Flex your stomach muscles against imagined G forces. Psychological studies have repeatedly shown that mental practicing like that can greatly increase your skill development rate and performance quality. Professional athletes do it. You can do it, too.

Learn at your best pace

Because learning aerobatic maneuvers can be mentally and physically taxing, you might not want to do all the maneuvers in each lesson during a single training flight. On the other hand, you might feel energized enough to try a maneuver slated for the next lesson. My curriculum organizes the sequence of maneuvers into lessons for the purpose of creating a logical and effective learning plan, but that does not mean that all the maneuvers in each lesson have to neatly fit into each training flight. Learn at your best pace, no matter what that pace is, and then you'll learn optimally, retain your skills longer, and have the most fun.

Clearing turns save lives

Be sure to make clearing turns before starting an aerobatic maneuver, or series of maneuvers. As soon as you leave straight-and-level, your flight path becomes unpredictable to other pilots in the area. You might soon be climbing toward them, diving or spinning at them, or doing a quick 180 into them. In other words, look up, down, and all around to make sure you have the practice area to yourself. Your clearing turn should be with a shallow or medium bank so you aren't distracted with coordinating a steep turn, or becoming susceptible to vertigo. Turn 360° or do two 180s. If you make a 360° turn with a high-wing airplane, roll out at the 180° point to reorient yourself and look under your wing for traffic before proceeding. If you want extra altitude, you can make a shallow climb while turning.

Maneuver entry altitude

The entry altitude your flight instructor recommends will depend on these factors:

- **FARs**. Review FAR 91.303 for legal requirements.
- **Performance**. Some airplanes climb faster and dive faster than other makes and models.
- **The maneuver**. Some maneuvers gain or lose more altitude than others. For example, a spin loses altitude and a roll generally doesn't.
- **Safety**. Some maneuvers are more prone to stall or spin upsets when pinched. For example, the relatively slow airspeed and high angle of attack on the backside of a loop can result in a stall or spin if you pull the stick back too hard—even though you are pointed straight down. Pushing too hard on the stick when inverted in an Immelmann can result in an outside stall or spin. Cross-controlling during the apogee (highest point) of a hammerhead turn can trigger an outside spin. All of these flubs are easily and quickly fixed when you learn how, but you still want a safety margin of extra altitude.

Throttle management

If your airplane does not have a constant speed propeller, you will often be retarding your throttle on downlines, and adding power on uplines. I don't talk about throttle placement in this book when describing maneuvers, but if you have a fixed pitch prop your instructor will brief you about throttle procedures during your flight training.

Who's flying?

Make sure you and your flight instructor have a clear procedure for handing off the airplane's controls. When I'm ready to demonstrate a maneuver or if I need to recover a botched maneuver for a confused student, I'll say "I've got the airplane." I'll wiggle the stick when I take it. When I want the student to take the controls, I'll say, "The airplane's yours." Tell your instructor that you heard and understood the instruction with "Okay, I've got it," or "Okay, it's yours."

Ground reference points

During your private pilot flight instruction, you practiced S-turns over a road and turns around a point on the ground to learn how to control the airplane's geographic path. You won't have to worry about wind corrections during recreational aerobatics, but ground references are still important for precision and spatial orientation. As an example, for a slow roll you'll pick a point of reference on the horizon and then roll around that point while keeping the nose equidistant from it. For a loop, you'll pick something like a straight road to make sure you exit the maneuver on the same heading that you entered it. If it's hard to find a specific point on the horizon for rolling maneuvers, just pick something significant, such as a distant town or landmark, or a distinctive terrain pattern. You'll check the horizon out of the side windows as a reference in some loop maneuvers to make sure your wings are level while inverted. I will suggest ground references for each maneuver described in this book's lesson plans.

Saying procedures aloud

When we get to the lesson on spins, you'll be instructed to always say the half-points out loud (*"Half, one, one and a half, two,"* and so on.) This will help you stay spatially oriented, and is especially important when the rotation rate speeds up. Cognitive research shows that when you say something aloud, it increases recall and focuses performance. For example, if you misplace your car keys and continuously say "keys, keys, keys" while going through your house looking for them, it can actually help. As another example, if you say "circle, circle, circle" while doing a slow roll around a point on the horizon, your automatic stick-and-rudder skills will better kick in to make the airplane's nose make an equidistant circle around the point.

Aborting a maneuver

If you ever get disoriented, or if you bungle a maneuver too much to fix it, just abort the maneuver and try it again. It's a waste of time and energy to try fixing something unfixable or unfathomable. For example, if you enter a loop with insufficient back pressure on the stick and feel the wings shuddering before you get inverted, you are not going to successfully complete a proper loop before stalling. Just lower the nose to pick up speed, roll right-side up, and start over.

Embrace your blunders

Errors are valuable learning experiences and contribute to your expertise—so feel good about making them. For example, when a student completes an aileron roll and exits the maneuver off-heading, it gives him an opportunity to explore ways to prevent that in the future. As a remedial exercise, for instance, I might have him fly another aileron roll, but without using any rudder. Seeing and feeling the resulting extreme adverse yaw will demonstrate the importance of adding enough rudder pressure to match aileron pressure. Or, I might tell that student to roll again, but this time use what seems like too much rudder. The usual result of that experiment is a properly coordinated roll, and an "Aha" learning moment for the student.

Knowledge + practice = competence

You'll get the most out of each training flight if you read the lesson plan for the scheduled maneuvers before coming to the airport. The "*How it's done, where to look*" steps will get you ready to fly each maneuver correctly.

Before getting into your airplane, use your hand or a toy airplane to show your instructor how you think each maneuver will look. This gives your CFI a chance to correct any misconceptions.

After your flight, take time at home to debrief your performance by re-reading the lesson plans for the maneuvers you flew. The "*Common errors and corrections*" tips will help you critique your performance, and think about improvements for next time.

In summary, when you combine your flight training with a few minutes of pre- and post-flight reading you will turbocharge your learning rate, retention, and confidence. You'll save time, money, and frustration. And, most importantly, you'll have more fun.

Note: You may download the flight lesson syllabus for this book at JamesLuger.com.

Thoughts for Instructors

During the pre-flight briefing, I use a toy airplane with about a 10-inch wingspan to show what the maneuver looks like, explaining control inputs and sight pictures while slowly moving the toy airplane around inside the hangar. Then I give the student the toy airplane and have him show how the maneuver should look in the air. Even though some maneuvers look different from inside the cockpit, this 3-D exercise seems to help students grasp the objective.

After reaching our practice area, I explain the maneuver one more time, and ask the student if he wants me to demonstrate it. Sometimes confident students decline the demonstration, and want try it on their own. I avoid distracting the student, but I will give brief simple-language pointers when needed: i.e., "Pull harder," or "Lots more rudder."

After completing the maneuver, I ask the student "What do you think about how that went?" I want the student to start analyzing her performance, diagnose problems, and think about solutions. She'll need those skills when practicing solo. The more mistakes she makes with me, the better, so I can help her recognize the problem and give her practices exercises that can remedy the problem.

Demonstrations can be helpful, but I think they can also be over-done. A demonstration doesn't let the student learn first-hand. Learning something new is hard and requires patience, especially if it's experiential, but when I take the controls to demo something, I'm not necessarily speeding up the learning process. My most important contribution is to be a watcher, an analyzer, a guide. I let students do as much of the flying as possible, within safe limits. I've had skilled stick and rudder pilots (i.e., ex-fighter pilots, bush pilots) learn every maneuver in the curriculum without me ever demonstrating a maneuver to them.

Demonstrating, however, does play an important instructional role. I almost always have to demonstrate a proper Lazy 8 and a barrel roll after students stumble through the first one. I explain what I am doing differently so they understand the comparison, and then let them try again. Sometimes a picture really is worth a thousand words.

Lesson 1 – Orientation Maneuvers

45° Up & Downlines, Chandelle, Lazy 8, Dutch Rolls, Competition Turns

The objectives of this lesson

1. Fly steep (45°) uplines and downlines to experience positive and negative G-loads while maintaining spatial orientation.
2. Manage the airplane's energy by converting altitude into speed and vice versa, and combining vertical lift with horizontal lift (a climbing turn with the Chandelle).
3. Coordinate ever-changing extreme pitch, roll, and control inputs throughout a complex maneuver (with the Lazy 8).
4. Managing throttle settings if the airplane does not have a constant speed propeller. (This will be an assumed factor in all proceeding lessons.)

Remember, this curriculum is based on accumulating successive skills. The skills you learn in one lesson will help you learn more challenging maneuvers in subsequent lessons. You'll eventually advance naturally, gradually and comfortably toward some of the most complex aerobatic maneuvers. So, let's start the fun with some important fundamentals.

1. 45-Degree Uplines and Downlines

The objective of this lesson is to experience a steep climb and steep descent, starting with a pullup G-load and then a slight floating sensation when pushing over the top. This will help you get used to mild physiological sensations, such as feeling heavy and then light, and flying unusually steep pitch angles with reference to the ground.

Reminder

Always make a thorough clearing turn before every maneuver or set of sequenced maneuvers described in this curriculum. Within the few seconds it took you to fly a particular maneuver, another pilot might have flown into your practice area. You are the unpredictable factor, so you need to make sure your practice airspace is clear in all directions.

How it's done, where to look

1. Start the maneuver at the aircraft's published maneuvering speed with cruise power, and pull up into a 45° climb. Pull with enough authority to feel heavier in your seat. How can you tell when the climb angle is 45°? Not by looking out the windshield because you'll only see blue sky and/or white clouds. You'll have to glance out a side window to see that your wings are about 45° in relation to the horizon. Quickly check the other side to make sure your wings are equidistant (equal distance) from the horizon.

2. When your controls feel light or mushy and your airspeed approaches stall speed, it's your signal to push the nose over into a 45° dive. Push with enough oomph to feel light in the seat, but not forcefully enough to pull you up against the seat belt. You can use your wingtips again as angle indicators, but since you'll be pointing toward the earth, can also estimate your 45° downline by aiming the nose at a point on the ground that's about halfway between straight-and-level, and straight down. That estimate will be amazingly accurate.

Common errors and corrections

Your instructor can give you feedback on how close your uplines and downlines were to a 45° angle. The remedy for angle errors is to glance at your wingtips on the way up, and at a ground reference on the way down. When reviewing this maneuver later, add a little excitement by pulling up a little harder into the climb, and pushing down more vigorously over the top. What might have started as an anxious new experience will soon get you smiling. I always feel a giggle in my tummy when I'm weightless, or nearly so. My grandkids love it, too.

Just do a couple of these for now. Don't overdo it on this first lesson. In fact, don't overdo anything on any lesson. Your aerobatic experiences will gradually train your brain and physiology to interpret anxiety as excitement, and then excitement as fun. When fun transforms into the pure joy of flight, you'll have achieved the realm of bird-like bliss. More about that lofty thought later.

A word about aerobatic sights

If you've ever seen a weird wire contraption either pointing back from an aerobatic airplane's wingtips or mounted on the struts, you might have mistaken it for some kind of exotic antenna that's large and complex enough to send messages into outer space. It's actually a sighting device. It helps aerobatic competitors accurately measure their aircraft's attitudinal relationship to the horizon. Think of it as a simple replacement for a gyro-controlled attitude indicator, which is either absent in aerobatic airplanes, or "caged" (locked in place) so it can't tumble uselessly out of control at the first sign of an extreme attitude. Competition pilots want to be spot-on with their attitudes because they are being scrutinized from the ground by fastidious judges who are keeping score. Such sighting aids, however, are not needed for aerobatic flight training because the simple estimating advice in this curriculum will give you close-enough attitude indications. Very few recreational aerobatic pilots bother with aiming devices for that reason, and many airshow pilots rely more on close-enough ground references because instead of being judged by trained observers on the ground, they want to put on an exciting show.

2. Chandelle

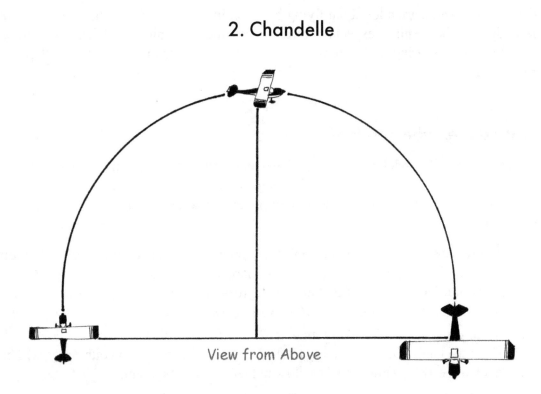

View from Above

French aerobatic pilot, Maurice Chevillard, was the first pilot to demonstrate what he called the *looping helicoidal*, a maneuver that maximized the rate of climb while turning 180°. The German World War I ace, Max Immelmann, later made this maneuver famous as a tactical maneuver, using it to attack his adversary from behind and then using the energy of momentum to turn and climb away. It was eventually and inexplicably renamed Chandelle (French for *candle*). Increasingly more exaggerated versions became possible when ailerons replaced the effective wing warping mechanisms used to induce rolls, and made possible an entirely new maneuver called the Immelmann turn. (You'll learn to perform the Immelmann later in this curriculum, after a few more preparatory skills are learned.)

For aerobatics, the Chandelle is a perfect exercise for optimizing energy management, a skill set that is more valuable to you than having a powerful engine, or for that matter, any engine at all. Many aerobatic maneuvers can be performed in aerobatic-designed gliders, using only energy management skills. The legendary aviator Bob Hoover did loops and rolls in a twin-engine Aero Commander with both engines turned off and the props feathered. Sometimes when I'm watching birds, especially birds of prey, I see them suddenly reverse directions and climb in elegant Chandelles, using only their wingtips for minor adjustments.

By the way, you can learn a lot about flying by watching birds. The Wright brothers spent hours studying airborne birds, especially birds of prey and water birds, which are the natural aviators that favor soaring and climbing on thermals rather than by constantly flapping their big wings.

How it's done, where to look

The objective of the Chandelle is to make a 180-degree turn while gaining as much altitude as possible. It can be performed with full power to maximize altitude gain, but we'll use cruise power to concentrate on the objective of managing aerodynamic energy with proper control inputs.

1. Before starting the maneuver, look for a point of reference either 90° to the left or right of your heading. Starting with maneuvering speed, roll the airplane into a medium-banked turn of 20° or 30° degrees, and immediately pull the airplane up into a gentle climbing turn. *Make sure you don't over-bank during the pullup.*

2. When you reach the 90° point, maintain the pitch attitude you have and gently roll out of the bank while continuing to climb, timing the rollout so your wings will be level at the 180° point. This is a slow maneuver, so be patient.

3. When you reach the point 180° from where you started, you should be on the verge of a stall, which would indicate you have maximized the climbing energy

available from your wings, power, and momentum to gain the maximum amount of altitude possible, all the while changing the direction of your flight 180°.

If this maneuver seems too tame to be an aerobatic maneuver, remember that all aerobatic maneuvers require careful energy management, and the Chandelle is the supreme maneuver to start building that skill set.

Common errors and corrections

- **Over-banking**. The most common error is over-banking during the pullup before reaching the 90° point. The airplane will want to over-bank, and you'll feel like you are cross-controlling to prevent it. Keep the bank at 20° or 30°, and coordinate your rudders to trim for adverse yaw (i.e., keep the inclinometer ball in the middle of the arc). If you over-bank, you are squandering horizontal (turning) lift, while sacrificing valuable vertical (climbing) lift.

- **Pitch too high**. If the pitch was too high at the 90° point, the airplane will run out of lift (i.e., stall) before you reach the 180° point. If the pitch was too low, you won't be gaining the maximum amount of altitude.

- **Rolling out too soon**. Reaching the 180° point before the wings are level. Roll out continuously and slowly. This maneuver requires timing, finesse, and patience.

- **Leftover speed**. Another common error is having too much speed left over at the 180° point. That extra speed could have been traded for more altitude gain.

- **Insufficient speed**. The opposite of too much speed at the end is not enough airspeed. It's fine if your wings are shuddering on the edge of a stall at the end, but if you enter a full stall, you'll give up valuable altitude in order to recover.

3. Lazy 8

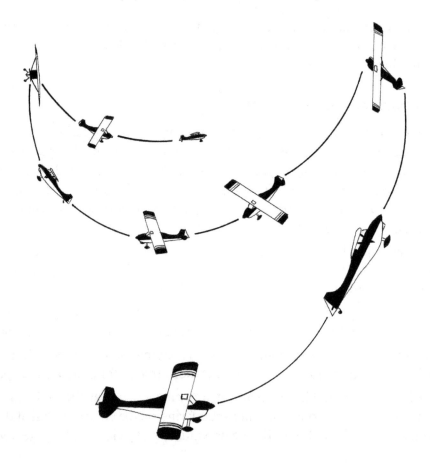

The aerobatic version of the Lazy 8 requires much steeper pitch changes and roll changes than the commercial pilot certification version. The aerobatic version of the Lazy 8 will help you increase your spatial orientation and precisely coordinate your control inputs during extreme attitude changes. The Lazy 8 is so named because it's a lazy-looking, elegant maneuver, beautiful to see from the ground and from inside the cockpit. Inside the cockpit, it will look like the nose is drawing a figure 8 in the sky, but from the ground it looks like a steep wing-over one way, and then another wingover the other way. (You should work through that difference for yourself on the ground sometime using a small toy airplane.) It's meant to be a coordinated maneuver with a low-G pullup, so you'll feel comfortable in your seat.

Simply put, you are going to turn the airplane 180 degrees from your starting point, while simultaneously and continuously changing the bank, roll, and pitch. When you reach your 180° point, you'll do the same thing in the other direction. You'll be busy on the stick and rudder, and when you can do one of these perfectly, you'll be demonstrating outstanding control of your aircraft.

How it's done, where to look

Use cruise power throughout. Look for an entry reference point on the horizon, and point your airplane's nose toward it. Look for another horizon reference point 90° degrees either right or left, depending on the direction of your entry turn (most right-handed pilots prefer left turns). Now look for a reference at the 45° point, and at the 135° point. Don't bother trying to find the 180° point for now because it's behind you and you can easily find it on the fly. (I do hope you like a pun now and then.) If you fly this maneuver over a straight road, it will be easy to stay oriented.

1. Start by rolling into a turn while at the same time applying back pressure on the stick to pitch up into a steep climb. Keep rolling, keep climbing.

2. **At the 45° point**, your nose will be at the highest pitch point (the higher the better), and your bank should be 45 degrees. Start lowering the nose but continue increasing the bank.

3. **At the 90° point**, your nose should drop through the horizon with a 90-degree bank ("knife edge"). Start rolling out, but let the nose continue pitching down into a dive. If your nose was high enough at the 45° point, you shouldn't pick up excessive airspeed in the dive.

4. **At the 135° point**, your aircraft's nose will be at the lowest point and your bank should be 45 degrees. Continue rolling out while pulling the nose up to your 180° point.

5. **At the 180° point**, your aircraft's attitude should be straight-and-level, and at your entry altitude. Now do the same thing in the other direction to complete the figure-8. Next time, do not pause at the 180° point to make it one continuous maneuver.

Here's a quick summary of your airplane's attitudes at each of the reference points:

Entry point – Straight and level.

45° point – 45° of bank, nose at its highest pitch.

90° point – 90° of bank, nose passing down through the horizon.

135° point – 45° of bank, nose at its lowest pitch.

180° point – Straight and level, immediately repeat in the other direction.

Whew! And you thought rubbing your tummy while patting your head was a big deal. Kidding aside, this maneuver is beautiful, lots of fun, and is a stick-and-rudder maneuver par excellence.

Common errors and corrections

Here are common flubs to watch for:

- **At the 45° point**, not having the pitch high enough. You need to bleed off airspeed with the nose pointing very high, otherwise you'll gain too much speed and lose too much altitude on the upcoming dive.

- **At the 90° point**, having less than a 90-degree bank. That can happen because knife edge flight might seem too radical to you at first. Another common error at this point is not continuing to push on the stick when the nose passes down through the horizon. Anticipate the nose needing to be at its lowest point at the 135° point.

- **At the 135° point**, not having the pitch low enough. You'll keep diving while gradually rolling out before reaching this point, and then continue rolling out while you pull the stick back hard enough to reach your entry altitude at the same time you reach the 180° point. Expect to feel a couple of Gs when you pull up from the 135° point to the 180° point.

Things happen faster after you pass through the horizon knife edged, but be patient with your control inputs. You might feel tempted to recover too soon from the accelerating dive, or you might want to roll out too soon.

4. Dutch Rolls

There are two versions of Dutch rolls. For jet aircraft, a Dutch roll is when an aircraft rolls in one direction and then the other, while yawing in the opposite direction—a hazardous loss of control configuration named after a Dutch speed skating technique (i.e., while weight goes to one skate, arms swing to the other side). In the propeller aircraft version, Dutch rolls are much more comfortable and safer. They are a series of coordinated rolls one way and then immediately the other way: roll right, roll left, roll right, and so on. You'll roll continuously back and forth while applying rudder in the same direction as the roll to counter adverse yaw—in other words, a coordinated roll. You'll need to bank back and forth quickly, maintaining forward momentum to prevent the airplane from entering a turn.

Because rolling maneuvers can trigger a bit of vertigo, especially at first, you should only do a couple of these with shallow or moderate banks for now. If you don't like them at all, then don't do them at all. It's like when a man went to the doctor and said it hurt when he pushed on a certain place on his arm. After a moment of reflection, the doctor said, "Then don't push on it." Don't fly Dutch rolls if they make you feel upset.

How it's done, where to look

1. First, pick a reference point on the horizon. Keep watching that point as you roll back and forth with shallow or medium banks, constantly changing from one side to the other. Your aircraft's nose should make an equidistant arc under the reference point.

2. Notice how you feel in your seat. If you feel pulled to one side or the other, you are either not applying enough rudder or applying too much rudder. If you feel centered in your seat, a quick glance at the inclinometer ball should confirm that your rolls are coordinated.

Don't gaze at the inclinometer ball, though. Keep your eyes outside the cockpit and don't worry about what the ball is doing. It's probably just sloshing back and forth with a delayed reaction, and you want to get used to keeping your eyes on your reference point. How you feel in the seat will become a more reliable coordination indicator than that brainless ball. There was a time in history when pilots didn't have an inclinometer, but they knew what it felt like to slip or skid in a turn.

The rudder's purpose in the air is a trim device to counter yawing from the greater drag on the downward aileron (the one on the rising wing). Lead with the ailerons and trim with the rudder—not the other way around—and your Dutch rolls will be comfortably yaw-free.

Dutch rolls are an excellent stick-and-rudder warm up before each lesson, as long as they don't make you woozy. They're like a baseball player's swinging of the bat a few times before the pitch. As you gain experience with Dutch rolls, gradually steepen your banks. See if you can go to 60° of bank.

Common errors and corrections

• **Losing your heading point**. If you roll one way and then delay rolling back to the other side, the airplane will start to turn and the nose will zoom past your reference point. As soon as you reach your desired medium bank of, say, 30°, *immediately* start rolling the other way. Momentum will keep you flying straight toward your point unless you delay reversing the bank.

- **Yawing**. Another common error is not using enough rudder while entering the roll, and not applying enough opposite rudder as soon as you start rolling the other way. Your stick will be constantly changing from side to side, so you need to coordinate those inputs with enough rudder to prevent adverse yaw.

- **Insufficient rudder**. If your airplane has an aileron-assist device (i.e., *spade or shovel*), you might feel like you are using too much rudder pressure to keep these rolls coordinated. That's because your ailerons have a wind-driven power assist, and your rudder does not. It also could be that, if you are new to aerobatics, you are not used to fast-changing rolls coordinated with fast and aggressive changing rudder pressure.

5. Competition Turns

A so-called competition turn is simply a brisk coordinated turn from one heading to another. It's meant to look snappy, the way a figure skater briskly enters the rink, or a gymnast struts out to begin her routine.

What makes competition turns different from normal turns is that you initiate it with a quick coordinated roll to your desired bank, and then immediately pull the airplane into the turn while maintaining the bank and altitude. When you reach your desired heading, stop the turn with forward pressure on the stick while rolling out. The rolls should be crisp and coordinated throughout the maneuver.

Dutch rolls will have prepared you for competition turns, but if you've done enough rolling for one day, you should practice competition turns during a future lesson. Too much rolling at first can mess with your physiology (more about that later in this book).

How it's done, where to look

1. Choose a point on the horizon to turn to. Quickly roll into a coordinated bank of 30°, but don't pull back on the stick yet because you don't want to start turning. (You can make the banks steeper after a little practice.)
2. Immediately upon reaching the 30° bank, pull back on your stick to initiate the turn. Use your ailerons to maintain that bank angle.
3. When you reach a desired point, stop the turn with quick forward pressure, then roll out. Keep the rollout coordinated with your rudder.

Common errors and corrections

- **Sluggish rolls**. Delaying your pull-back after establishing your initial bank will make the turn entry less dramatic. Make it brisk and crisp.

- **Overbanking**. When you pull back on the stick to make the turn, the airplane might try to over-bank. Counter accordingly with your aileron.

- **Uncoordinated**. Because the control movements must be made in quick succession, you'll have to be quick on the rudders to keep the turn coordinated. This is NOT a cross-controlled maneuver. It should be made with enough rudder input to keep it coordinated throughout.

- **Altitude loss**. As with all turns, you are trading some vertical lift for horizontal lift, so you'll need to watch the nose in relation to the horizon to keep enough back pressure on the stick. You want to maintain your altitude throughout the turn, but you'll be busy maintaining your bank angle with the increased backpressure.

- **Misused as a clearing turn**. Competition turns are NOT meant for clearing turns because managing the maneuver keeps you distracted from a thorough search for nearby traffic. It is also not an official aerobatic competition maneuver. It's meant to be a snappy turn-around when the required maneuver sequence requires a change in direction. In short, it's just to look cool.

Lesson 1 Thoughts for Instructors

My overall objective for Lesson 1 is to introduce some new flight attitudes, sight pictures, and physiological feelings to the student. I want students to see what knife-edge flight looks like in the Lazy 8, feel more than one G pulling up to the 45 upline, feel less than one G when tipping over into the 45° downline, and experience the need for aggressive aileron and rudder inputs in Dutch rolls and competition turns. If you've been teaching aerobatics, you know that's a real first-lesson workout for most students.

I don't think exact precision is a priority at this stage, so I don't use up the student's cognitive resources by repeating Chandelles and Lazy 8s ad nauseam. I keep close watch on the student's well-being. I take time to chat about the maneuver, sight-see and enjoy the flight. Actually, I seldom introduce all of these maneuvers in Lesson 1. I often leave Dutch rolls and competition turns for a future lesson. If the student starts getting quiet and lacks responsiveness on the controls, I declare the mission a success and we return victoriously to the airport. I find that empathy for the student is an important mentoring tool.

51

At the end of this book, I'll give you a website link where you can download the entire syllabus of this curriculum. I print one for each student, and I keep a copy for each student as a training log, with performance notations, flight time, and date.

Working with once-traumatized students

I've sometimes had students who tell me about some aerobatic pilot that gave them a harrowing aerobatic ride, maybe with the intention of getting the student excited about aerobatics. Those students typically went home feeling sick, and vowed to never go through something that frightening again. Years later, a pilot like this sometimes musters enough courage to try overcoming his fear, by learning how to perform aerobatic maneuvers from a competent aerobatic CFI. My first lesson with such a student will be little more than steep uplines and downlines, a Chandelle, and if all goes well with those maneuvers, ask him if he'd like me to demo his choice of a simple aileron roll or a loop. If he says yes, and likes it, I'll invite him to perform one. I'll give feedback, but I never judge a student's performance as good or bad. After that we fly back to the airport and rightfully declare the mission a success. I want that pilot to 1) have fun, which flying should be; 2) leave with a sense of accomplishment and confidence, and 3) feel enthusiastic about returning for more. What could be more successful on a first lesson than that?

Lesson 2 – Flying Upside Down

Aileron Roll and Loop

The objectives of this lesson

1. Learn additional fundamental building block maneuvers that will help you master virtually all other "inside" (positive G-force) non-spin aerobatic maneuvers.
2. Coordinate control inputs during a primary aileron roll.
3. Experience G-forces and maintain spatial orientation during a loop.
4. Learn to precisely fly extreme attitude angles by using ground references.

Review Suggestions

Either a Dutch roll or competition turn

Either a chandelle or Lazy 8

During Lesson 1, you learned energy management with the Chandelle, spatial orientation with the Lazy 8, and experienced G-force changes with 45° uplines and downlines. In this lesson, you'll learn a basic aileron roll and a loop, and you'll put those maneuvers together in various ways in subsequent lessons to learn more complex maneuvers and combinations. You'll also make assertive control inputs to change attitudes, and learn to identify high angles of attack when your control responses become sluggish.

An aileron roll is a good inverted flight maneuver to start with because it's coordinated (aileron and rudder inputs to the same side), pulls almost no increased G-forces inside or out (a bit of centrifugal force keeps you comfortably in your seat), and errors almost never result in some kind of upset (like a spinout, inverted dive, or a tail slide).

As with the aileron roll, a loop gives you a taste of another fundamental maneuver that was born of the ever-expanding limits of early chandelles.

1. Aileron Roll

Early pilots tried unsuccessfully to "capsize" their airplanes into inverted flight by rolling over, but banking with wing warping systems gave them only enough rolling power to reach knife edge before the heavy nose dropped into a vertical dive. Aerobatic pilots knew how to half-loop and then continue flying inverted from the top of the loop, but they recovered by diving from inverted and pulling upright under heavy G-load—a maneuver now called a split-S. But when pilots finally learned how to half-roll from inverted flight, they had a way to return upright without a split-S. This minimized altitude loss and reduced G-force stress on the airplane, which was a danger then with split-S pullouts, and still is today. The rollout from inverted was possible because the weight of the heavy upside-down wheels pointing skyward helped the airplane roll over to right-side up, but the weight of those wheels hanging down would have to be overcome before pilots could roll from upright to inverted. That required the invention of ailerons, which were much more effective than wing warping, and could reliably roll the airplane completely around.

To perform an aileron roll, you will use full aileron deflection to roll the aircraft all the way around to return upright. You will keep the roll coordinated by using rudder pressure—in fact, quite a lot of rudder pressure in most aerobatic trainers.

How it's done, where to look

1. Pick out a reference point on the horizon and fly toward it with the power setting recommended by your airplane's POH. (Usually cruise power.)

2. When your aircraft is at the recommended aileron roll airspeed, pull the nose up to about 20° above the horizon. Momentarily ease off on the stick's back pressure to stop the nose from going any higher.

3. Immediately add full aileron deflection to one side, and coordinate the roll by pressing the rudder on the same side.

4. After rolling 360° with the wings back to straight and level flight, remove aileron and rudder inputs. Your nose should be pointing to your reference point on the horizon. You won't make a circle around that point with the nose, however, because

the initial pullup brought the nose straight up from the reference point. The nose, therefore, will make a "D" pattern around your reference point instead of a circle. (You'll be learning the more-challenging slow roll later in this curriculum, with which you will make a complete circle around your point on the horizon.)

Common errors and corrections

- **Sustained back pressure on the stick**. If you bring the nose up and fail to "unload" the wings by releasing backpressure at about 20° above the horizon, the aircraft will try to "climb" throughout the roll. That will make the maneuver more of a sloppy barrel roll (more about those later), than a crisp aileron roll. You'll also end up with more speed than you want because backpressure on the stick when inverted pulls your nose into an inverted dive. I'll untangle possible confusion about that in a moment.

- **Sluggish roll rate**. If you pause too long after easing off the stick with the nose 20° above the horizon, your airspeed will quickly erode and the roll will be sluggish. Start your roll as soon as you've momentarily paused about 20° above the horizon.

- **Exited off-heading**. If the nose doesn't end up at your original reference point, you might not have neutralized the rudder while neutralizing the ailerons. You also might have used too much rudder pressure during the roll, but it's more likely that you didn't use enough. When you are new to aerobatics, using a sufficient amount of rudder pressure in a roll can feel like it's excessive. If you have trouble with this, ask your instructor if you can roll without any rudder to experience how extreme the yaw feels, and see how the nose slides away from the reference point when recovering. Then roll in the same direction with more rudder than you think is necessary. When I ask students which version (with more rudder or with less rudder) they like best, they realize the need for lots of rudder whenever using lots of aileron.

How Inverted Flight Affects Control Inputs

Do I push or pull to go up or down when right-side up or upside down?

Huh? That paragraph headline is a parody about how proper stick inputs can be confusing when flying inverted. Back pressure while right-side-up will, of course, pull the nose up away from the earth, but when you are upside-down, backpressure pulls the nose downward toward the earth. That's fairly easy to comprehend when you have a moment to ponder it, but there's a speedier memory tag. Just remember that when you pull back on the stick, the nose will always move toward your head, and when you push the stick, the nose will always move toward your feet. This rule works whether you are flying right-side up, upside down, straight up, straight down, or sideways. (But not backward. We'll discuss tailslide recoveries later.)

Adverse (opposing) yaw revisited

Before leaving this topic of rolling, let's revisit *adverse yaw*, a term you were introduced to when you started to learn how to fly. But other than holding right rudder against P-factor during your climb, how much attention do you really give to the rudder? Not much if you are like most non-aerobatic pilots. At least that's what I've found while lightly monitoring rudder inputs with my feet during new aerobatic students' first lessons. I'm sure it's because in the everyday right-side-up realm of gradually entering shallow or moderate banks, you can under-rudder with little noticeable consequence. I used to teach primary flying, and when students initiated a bank, I'd often have to say "Remember your rudder," or "Check the ball."

But adverse yaw will be more pronounced in aerobatic flying, so let's take a moment to appreciate why. As you know, when you use your ailerons, one goes up to make the airstream against it push that wing down, and when the other aileron goes down the airstream against it pushes that wing up. But those wind deflection pressures are not equal. That's because, non-technically speaking, the airstream blows straighter across the bottom of the wing because the underside is generally flatter than the curved topside (camber differential). That makes the wing with the down-aileron catch more wind, which gives it more lift, but also more drag. The airplane's nose is pulled toward the side with the most drag (the side opposite of the turn direction), which is called adverse yaw. This problem is exacerbated during maneuvers when you rapidly apply full aileron, something you don't do when flying cross-country or in the airport pattern.

How the rudder was invented to fix adverse yaw is an interesting story.

The Wright Brothers used a rudder, but not as a turning device. They fixed a pair of rudders to the back-end of their Wright Flyer strictly as an adverse yaw trim device. Many competing airplane inventors of the time thought of rudders as turning devices because boats used them for that purpose—and, as the logic ran, air is like thin water. But Orville and Wilber were avid bird watchers, so they knew banking was nature's solution to turning something that flew in a three-dimensional environment. (That applied to bicycles, as well.) They used cables to "warp" (increase) the camber of a wing so it would lift into a banked turn. So far, so good. But sustained flight was hampered because the warped wing created so much drag, that the nose yawed toward it, opposite of the intended turn direction. Installing moveable rudders to push the nose back into the turn solved the problem, as rudders still do today.

2. Loop

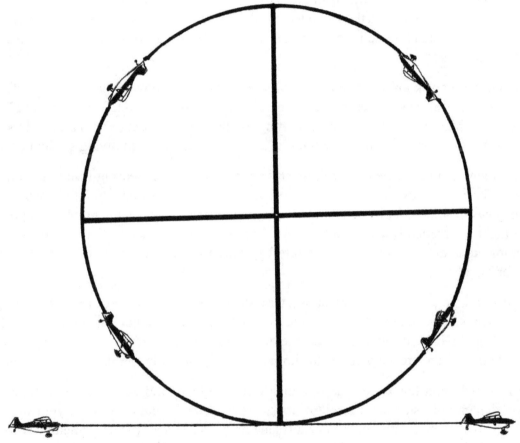

The term, "loop" came from a popular early 1900s fairground ride that used descending momentum and centrifugal force to make its railcars loop up and over inverted and then dive to upright on other side. Promoters hawked the exciting ride as "looping the loop."

When early pilots first tried to perform a loop-the-loop in an airplane, they either broke something on the airplane (i.e., a wing) or ended up in an "unrecoverable" (at least believed so at the time) stall, spin, or worse, the dreaded highspeed "graveyard spin" (a spiral—more about those later).

On September 1, 1913, French pilot, Adolphe Pegöud demonstrated the first aerial loop in his 50hp Bleriot XI. He began the loop in front of a crowd of spectators at an altitude of just over 3,000 feet, first reducing the engine to idle, then pushing the "steering pillar" to nose over into a dive for entry speed. When Pegöud felt the airspeed was sufficient, he pulled up into inverted straight-and-level flight. After waving at his onlookers while reportedly traveling inverted for about a thousand feet, he dove again and recovered from the remaining half-loop. (As a stand-alone maneuver, the second half of a loop from sustained inverted flight is now called a split-S.)

Although everyone knows what a loop is, you might not know how to make a loop perfectly round. You'll also need to learn how to quickly and easily recover from "pinching" the maneuver, which means stalling from pulling too hard on the stick, with an already steep angle of attack. You can stall at any point in a loop, including when diving straight down.

As with any looping maneuver, you must first make a careful clearing turn that includes looking for traffic above you and below you because you'll be using a lot of airspace. Start the maneuver with enough altitude to recover safely from any flubs, but not so high that you might inadvertently fly up into a cloud or controlled airspace. Your instructor will recommend an entry altitude for the aircraft you are flying, and might add a few hundred feet for safety.

If you live in one of the central or western states, you'll probably find a nice straight government survey road to fly over, which will give you a reference line to look for when you go from inverted through the backside of the loop. If you don't have any straight roads below you, find a reference point on the horizon to look for while completing the maneuver.

You'll be pulling a few Gs on the first quarter of the loop, and again on the last quarter. If you tighten your stomach muscles during heavy G-loads (but don't hold your breath), you'll feel more comfortable. If your airplane has a "G-meter" (accelerometer), you can glance at it during the initial pullup to make sure you are pulling enough Gs to make it all the way around. (For the Super Decathlon I fly, about 4 Gs with two people aboard is about right during the first and last quarters of the loop.) After a bit of practice, you'll be able to feel whether you're pulling the correct G-load.

During the top of the loop, you won't be hanging from your seatbelt because of centrifugal force. It's like swinging a bucket with some water in it. The water stays at the bottom throughout the swing because of centrifugal force.

58

How it's done, where to look

1. **Before beginning the loop**, you might have to dive a bit to reach the entry speed recommended for loops in the aircraft's POH. If you have a fixed-pitch propeller, add in full power during the first half of the loop, and reduce the throttle to idle for the last half of the loop. If you have a constant-speed prop, then leave the throttle at the cruise setting. (During the remainder of this curriculum, I won't discuss throttle changes for fixed pitch airplanes, but, in short, add power when you climb, reduce power when you dive. Your flight instructor will advise you about the specifics for each maneuver in the airplane you will be training in.)

2. **During the first quarter of the loop**, apply enough back pressure on the stick to feel heavy in your seat. You'll be pulling against gravity *and* centrifugal force, so expect to pull hard and feel heavy. If you have a G-meter, your instructor will tell you how many Gs to pull for the airplane you are training in. If your nose yaws during the pullup it's probably because of P-factor (asymmetrical disk loading) and gyroscopic effect from the propeller, in which case add enough right rudder (for American aircraft) to trim for it. Yawing will be more pronounced in shorter airplanes, like the Pitts Special, and less pronounced with long fuselage airplanes (because of more leverage) like the Super Decathlon.

3. **During the second quarter of the loop,** begin to relax a little back pressure. You'll still be pulling, though, to maintain centrifugal force. If you push on the stick, you'll stop looping and simply fly inverted. When your aircraft becomes fully inverted, relax a little more back pressure, and glance at both wingtips to make sure they are equidistant (equally distant) in relation to the horizon.

4. **During the third quarter of the loop**, start adding backpressure to maintain centrifugal force. You won't need to pull hard because gravity will help you by tugging on the heavy nose. You'll be diving steeply, so your airspeed will increase quickly. Glance through the ceiling window or canopy to look for that straight road or horizon point for a directional reference.

5. **When you enter the fourth quarter of the loop**, start pulling hard again, as heavily as you did during the first quarter. In addition to centrifugal force, you are overcoming gravitational pull. As your speed picks up past cruise speed, you might have to add a bit of left rudder to trim for what I'll call "negative P-factor." (Airplanes are designed with the vertical stabilizer offset to overcome P-factor yaw during cruise speed. It won't be offset enough during a climb, however, so you'll need to add right rudder when you climb. Likewise, the offset vertical stabilizer will be too much counterforce above cruise speed, as in a dive, so you'll might have to add left rudder to compensate.)

Common errors and corrections

The most common mistake is making an egg-shaped (ovoid) loop. The second most common mistake is recovering at an altitude that is higher or lower than your entry altitude, and a close third flub is exiting at a different heading than your entry heading. Stalling during the loop happens less frequently. Here's how to prevent and fix these errors.

- **An ovoid instead of a circle**. Until you refine your spatial orientation skills, your instructor will tell you if your loop was egg-shaped. The simple prevention is to relax a little more backpressure (but don't push on the stick) for a couple of seconds while inverted, and start increasing backpressure when the nose drops into the third quarter of the loop.

- **If you exited higher than your starting altitude**, you either pulled too hard during the last two quarters of the circle, or you didn't release enough back pressure while rounding over the top.

- **If you exited at an altitude lower than your entry**, you either didn't relax enough backpressure on top to reduce airspeed, or you didn't pull back hard enough during the first or third quarters. When you're new to aerobatics, pulling anything more than a couple of Gs feels unnatural. Tighten your stomach muscles during G-loads, and rest assured you'll soon get used to them.

- **You might have recovered with a wing low**, probably accompanied by an off-heading exit. A wing dipped somewhere during the maneuver, most likely while you were inverted on top of the loop, and stayed that way for the rest of the maneuver. By the way, trying to correct with a quick yaw back to the entry heading will not fool your instructor— aerobatic instructors can feel when an airplane is trying to fly sideways. The best place to check for uneven wings is while inverted on top of the loop, when things are happening a little slower and you have an easy view of the horizon. Simply glance at one wing tip and then the other to make sure the wings are equidistant from the horizon. If not, make a quick aileron input to fix it.

- **If you relaxed too much backpressure when inverted**, you might have felt a bit weightless, or like you were hang by your seatbelt. You need to keep some backpressure throughout the maneuver to avoid flattening the top of the loop and losing too much airspeed.

- **It's possible to enter a stall or spin** anywhere during a loop, but especially on the top or on the backside. Your warning might be nothing more than slight buffeting of the wings and mushy response from your control inputs. I've watched many students who have stalled during a loop instinctively try to recover by pulling back harder on the stick, and even more aggressively when it doesn't bring the nose up. You already know that more backpressure on the stick deepens the angle of attack, and that reducing backpressure fixes it. But when things don't make immediate sense, it throws your cognitive awareness for a loop (I couldn't resist the pun). Even though you had training in stall recognition and recovery during primary and advanced flight training, feeling stall symptoms when the nose is pointing more or less straight down can seem bewildering at first. Your reflex reaction might be to try to pull out of what looks like a severe dive. Psychologists call this temporary denial of reality "post cognitive dissidence." You'll learn more about PCD and other interesting physiological gremlins when we get to the multi-turn spin lessons.

If all this stall and spin talk is making you nervous, I have good news for you. This curriculum, along with flight training by a competent aerobatic certified flight instructor, will teach you to anticipate, identify, and recover from a variety of what is commonly called "upsets." This is a perfect segue into the next lesson, which is about recognizing imminent stalls and spins, and if they happen, how to recover quickly, safely, and with minimum altitude loss.

More good news: spins in aerobatic airplanes are safe at a safe altitude, and are a lot of fun!

Lesson 2 Thoughts for Instructors

If a student begins to stall during this lesson, I simply mention we're stalling. If he doesn't recover, I'll tell him to relax backpressure. If the stall deepens and a wing starts to dip, I'll coach him through the recovery. But if the student seems confused, or if the stall progresses into an incipient spin, I'll tell him that I've got the controls.

As long as we have plenty of altitude, I'd rather have the student identify and recover from the stall. If he sorts out and fixes the problem with my guidance, it becomes an indelible learning moment.

I advise all students to refrain from practicing loops solo until after the next lesson, which focuses on stall and spin recovery.

Lesson 3 – Essential Recovery Skills

Slow Flight, Stall, Spin

Objectives of this lesson

1. Recognize imminent stall indications while flying at minimum controllable airspeed (MCA), with and without power.
2. Enter and recover from a stall while using rudders to avoid spinning.
3. Enter a spin and recover with minimum altitude loss.

During this lesson, you'll learn to recognize an excessive angle of attack (AOA) and insipient (forming, early stage) stalls and spins. You will also learn to recover reflexively, precisely, and immediately.

By the way, a goal of stall and spin recoveries in this curriculum will always call for a minimum loss of altitude. You want that to be your default automatic reflex in case a stall or spin takes you by surprise. That reflexive skill, however, can be set aside when you later practice secondary stalls or multiple-turn spins, or during competition when the recovery calls for a vertical downline, but those incidents should be exceptions to your standard recovery procedure.

Note: You should always recover from stalls and spins according to the airplane manufacturer's recommended procedures in the pilot operating handbook (POH) if those recommendations differ from the descriptions in this curriculum.

Review Suggestions

Brief Dutch roll warmup (unless they are unsettling)

Loop

Aileron roll to the left and to the right

1. Minimum Controllable Airspeed

You should already know that stalls result from an excessive angle of attack, and not necessarily the result of low airspeed, even though the manufacturer's pilot's operating handbook (POH) publishes stall airspeeds. If a pilot yanks back hard enough on the stick while at speeds well above the published stall speed, the angle of attack can instantly become great enough to stall the airplane. For example, when learning snap rolls (i.e., horizontal accelerated spins) later in this curriculum, you'll be stalling/spinning at considerably higher airspeed than the POH's published stall speed. By the way, you can stall without a spin, but you can't spin without a stall. The spin results when one wing is stalled deeper than the other wing.

Because flying at ever-lower speeds increases the angle of attack, and puts you ever-closer to a stall, we'll practice minimum controllable airspeed (MCA, or "slow flight") to get you use to the mushy response of your controls. If you become sensitized to an imminent stall, you are less likely to let it happen.

How it's done, where to look

1. Pick a reference point on the horizon, and with flaps up (if you have them), reduce power to idle.
2. Increase back pressure on the stick to maintain your altitude. Use your right rudder to trim against P-factor yaw, and gently bank as needed to keep the airplane's nose lined up with your reference point.
3. When your airspeed approaches stall speed, add just enough power to maintain that speed and altitude. Keep your wings level and correct any P-factor yawing with your rudders.
4. When you've stabilized your airplane at MCA, make a shallow turn one way to a point 90° from your reference point and roll out. Then roll back to your reference point and roll out.
5. Add power back to cruise, and maintain your direction and altitude while the airplane returns to cruise speed.

Common errors and corrections

- **Not achieving MCA.** If you maintain an airspeed above MCA, you won't feel how unresponsive the controls are just before reaching critical angle of attack, which is when the airstream starts flowing roughly over the rear top of the wings.

Being on the edge of a stall can make you feel uneasy, but if the airplane stalls, it won't fall out of the sky. Just dip the nose down and let the wings catch air again.

- **Going below MCA**. If the airplane stalls, your speed got too low for the configuration you're in. Dip the nose and add power to recover.

2. Idle-Power Stall

You practiced stalls to earn your pilot's certificate, but this exercise lets you experience them in the airplane in which you are taking your aerobatic flight training.

For the sake of clear communication, I use the term "idle power" instead of "power off," which could mean turning the engine off. I use the term "add power" instead of "power on" because the power is already on when the engine is idling.

Most modern general aviation aircraft will have a slightly higher angle of incidence near the root of the wing, a design feature called "washout." This is to give your ailerons some control authority during the first indication of a stall. It also means the air over the thicker, highest lift portion of the wing will start to burble and buffet first, which gives you advance warning. I realize that your airplane will have an audible stall warner, but what if it's not working? You want to detect an imminent stall early by feeling the wings buffeting and from reduced control responsiveness.

Airplanes that do not have wing washout include some antique airplanes and advanced aerobatic airplanes. Those airplanes will immediately break into a full stall or spin as soon as the critical angle of attack is exceeded, an advantage in some advanced aerobatic maneuvers.

If the airplane's POH describes stall recoveries in ways that differ from the descriptions below, use the POH's recovery instructions instead.

How it's done, where to look

1. Pick a reference point on the horizon and keep your airplane pointed in that direction with level wings. Reduce power to idle.
2. Gradually pull back on the stick back to maintain your altitude. Correct any yawing with opposite rudder and use gentle banks to keep wings level and on point.
3. When the wings buffet and the nose begins to drop, recover by pushing the stick forward enough to reduce angle of attack (push to neutral or just past neutral on most airplanes—consult the POH for the airplane you are flying) and then add power to cruise while bringing the nose back to straight and level flight.

Common errors and corrections

- **Recovering too soon.** If you recover at the first sign of buffeting, you're wing might not have been fully stalled. You should always recover at this point if the stall was not intended, but in this practice, you want to feel how the airplane behaves when fully stalled.

- **Recovering too late**. If the nose aggressively pitches downward, you have allowed the stall to develop too deeply. This is an error in this lesson because the objective is to recover with a minimum loss of altitude. Recover as soon as the stall is detected but not fully developed.

- **Not keeping maintaining the heading**. If your wings are not level, your nose will turn away from your reference point. If your wings *are* level and your nose creeps to one side of you reference point, then you are yawing. You correct yawing by pushing the opposite rudder, or ease off a rudder if you are pushing it too much.

- **Entering an unintended secondary stall.** If you pull back the stick too hard and/or too soon when recovering from the stall, you could increase the angle of attack enough to stall again. In that case, lower the nose enough to recover from the second stall, add power while bringing the nose up carefully while airspeed increases.

3. Spin

A quick spin history lesson

Before World War I, the spin was called a "spiral dive." Later in this book, you'll learn the characteristics and recovery differences between a spiral and a spin, but from the ground and inside the cockpit both maneuvers look similar. We'll concentrate on spins in this lesson, which requires a stalled wing, whereas a spiral does not.

The unfortunate early pilots who found themselves in a spin never survived to tell how they tried to recover, but aghast spectators on the ground would sometimes see the hapless pilot pulling back on the control stick with all his might, and pushing the stick in the opposite direction of rotation. But to no avail. Getting into a spin in those early days of aviation was simply a death sentence.

But in August of 1912, British Lt. Wilfred Parke inadvertently found himself in a spin and lived to tell about it. When his aircraft went out of control, he did all the wrong things that other pilots had instinctively tried (and, sadly, so do modern pilots who were not trained in spin recovery). Lt. Parke pulled full back on the stick to break the dive and tried to roll out of the spin with full opposite ailerons, both of which made the spin worse. Afraid of being catapulted from his open cockpit in the steep turning dive, Lt. Parke let go of the control stick to grab onto the airplane's interior struts. Then, without any reason except that he had tried everything else, he pushed the rudder that was opposite of the spin direction. The airplane, now only about 50 feet above the ground, according to witnesses, instantly stopped spinning and flattened out with very little further altitude loss. He circled the field he was over, and made a normal landing. When Lt. Parke revealed his life-saving recovery control inputs to the pilots of the world, the incident became known as Parke's Dive. Since then, pilots who received spin recovery training acquired the skills that, when altitude allowed, would allow them to successfully recover from spins. After you receive flight training for this lesson, you'll be one of those fortunate pilots.

Letting go of the controls

Most modern airplanes will eventually recover from an inside spin on its own if you let go of the stick and rudder controls (see research done by German pilot Eric Müller and American pilot Gene Beggs). This lesson, however, describes an assertive recovery procedure that minimizes altitude loss. You want an effective, reflexive skill-set in place in case a spin ever takes you by surprise.

Inadvertent spins

You will be practicing stalls and spins briefly at this point in the curriculum because it's possible to inadvertently enter a spin even from a simple loop. The initial practice will be brief, however, so you don't get worn out doing them. Later in the curriculum you'll perform increasingly more advanced stalls and spins. By the way, an ideal time to perform a spin is at the end of each lesson to lose altitude before returning to the airport traffic area.

A bit of science

In summary, a spin can result when one wing is more deeply stalled than the other wing. This can happen if the airplane yaws at the onset of, or during, a stall. Yawing one direction with your rudder will increase the speed and lift of the wing on the side opposite of your pushed rudder, while decreasing the speed and lift of the wing on the side of your pushed rudder. If the differential is great enough, the faster wing will increase its lifting power, and the slower wing will lose its lifting power and decrease its airspeed enough to stall. Hence, the high-lift wing chases the low-lift stalled wing around and around, which is called *autorotation*. They probably don't explain it this way in aeronautical engineering schools, but I think this explanation accurately unbundles the science, and it's a quick and accurate sketch of what we see and experience from the cockpit.

You can spin during any flight configuration, such as while inverted or when pointing straight down (like during the backside of a loop), and you can spin during airspeeds that are higher than the manufacturer's published stall speed. An example would be a snap roll, where full, brisk rudder and stick deflection puts the airplane into an immediate accelerated horizontal spin from straight-and-level flight. (You'll learn about snap rolls later in this book.)

Spin recovery procedure

You'll see in this lesson that a spin is a procedural, timing maneuver. You are either in a spin or you're not, and if you are, you follow a procedure to recover. In contrast, while flying a loop, for instance, your performance can be anywhere from sloppy to perfect, and you can fix problems during the loop, or abort the maneuver in a number of ways.

The P-A-R-E procedure

For any spin recovery, you want a reflexive reaction like the below "**PARE**" procedure shown below. (Use the spin recovery recommended in your airplane manufacturer's pilot operating handbook (POH) if it differs from the below recovery procedure.)

P – **Power** to idle (power can raise the nose up into a flat spin, or delay recovery).

A – **Ailerons** neutral (ailerons extended can aggravate the spin and delay recovery).

R – **Rudder** applied fully in the opposite direction of the spin.

E – **Elevator** pushed* to, or a bit past, neutral (as recommended in the POH) to reduce the angle of attack.

Practice PARE with your homemade simulator

The PARE acronym is only useful for mentally and/or physically rehearsing spin recoveries while on the ground. If an unintended spin catches you by surprise, you won't have time to think through all the steps—you'll need to apply them reflexively and immediately. To

---

* The elevator will be pulled past neutral if you are in an outside spin. More about outside spins later.

make that possible, your spin recovery procedure should be simulated on the ground until it is intuitive and fast. To practice, I suggest that you sit in a chair or in the cockpit, and move your hands and feet while saying the name of the PARE control aloud, like this:

"Power…ailerons…rudder…elevator."

You can just touch the throttle (or imaginary throttle) for the "power" action. Practice this a few times until you can quickly apply the entire PARE procedure within 2 or 3 seconds. The power, ailerons, and rudder inputs should be done simultaneously. Mental rehearsal combined with actual practice will help you instinctively recover with minimal altitude loss. You'll enter intentional spins with the power already at idle, but you'll probably enter an unintended spin with the power higher. Practicing on the ground will help you include immediately bringing the power to idle during an actual spin upset.

Keep track of rotations

There's a second procedural, timing aspect to spins. During an intentional spin, you should keep track of your turns by counting half-turns out loud. For example, *"half, one, one-and-a-half, two,"* etc. Count this way aloud even when you practice spins solo. When you practice multiple-turn spins, you'll see how counting helps you keep track when the spin rate increases.

During this lesson, you'll recover as soon as the spin begins, just enough to see the effects of the controls. It will be a brief early-stage spin, but you'll be able to see how much the nose moved off your heading, and note how much altitude you lose before recovering.

It's okay to wait

If practicing slow flight and stalls during this lesson has already challenged your tolerance, either tell your instructor you'd like to take a short sight-seeing break (looking ahead, not straight down), or that you're ready to return to the airfield. This curriculum advocates learning maneuvers in a certain sequence, but that doesn't mean you have to complete all the maneuvers listed in any give lesson. If you don't feel up to doing one of the maneuvers, do it in the next lesson. The goal is to maintain your best learning rate, and the way to measure that is to notice how you feel. If you're having fun, your learning rate is optimum. If you feel overloaded, you should call the training mission a success, and start where you left off in the next flight lesson.

How it's done, where to look

1. Establish a specific direction, either a compass heading or point on the horizon. Start at an altitude recommended by your flight instructor. As always, make a thorough clearing turn, all around and up and down.

2. While flying straight-ahead, reduce power to idle. Use enough back pressure on the stick to maintain altitude.

3. At the first indication of a stall, immediately push full rudder to either side and pull the stick fully straight back. *Keep your ailerons neutral* throughout the maneuver—holding the stick back with both hands might help to keep it centered.

4. As soon as a wing drops and the nose begins to move off your heading, add full opposite rudder. As soon as the rotation slows or stops, return the stick position forward to just past neutral (or whatever position your aircraft's POH recommends.)

5. As soon as you recover from the spin and stall, add power to cruise while adding enough backpressure to bring the nose back to straight-and-level flight.

6. After resuming normal flight, notice how much you deviated from your entry heading, and how much altitude you lost.

Common errors and corrections

- **A hasty clearing turn**. Make a medium-bank, 180° turn while looking all around, and up and down. Then continue around to your original heading. You'll be spinning straight down, and any aircraft under you will not see you coming. Your sudden change in heading, altitude, and attitude will make you unpredictable to traffic around you. It's up to you to spot and avoid other aircraft.

- **Abrupt control inputs.** When it's time to add rudder and back pressure, add them fully and with authority, but don't ever *kick* the rudder or *yank* the stick back because that's hard on the airplane, and you might snap into an aggressive spin entry. You'll be practicing accelerated stalls and spin recoveries later in this curriculum because they might take you by surprise if you inadvertently stall during a maneuver. For now, however, recovering from an initial (incipient) spin is the goal.

- **Delayed recovery.** When it's time to recover from a spin, recover immediately with full opposite rudder, and swiftly move the stick forward. When airspeed starts to increase, add cruise power while bringing the airplane out of the dive. You are developing a habit of minimizing your altitude loss in case an unintended stall or spin ever takes you by surprise.

- **Secondary stall.** If you pull out of the recovery dive too abruptly, you could increase the angle of attack enough to stall again, even though your nose is pointed downward. Pull firmly but gradually as airspeed increases, while adding power back to cruise.

Lesson 3 thoughts for Instructors

I've found that the reason new aerobatic students sometimes feel uncomfortable about stalls and spins is because the student's primary training CFI was nervous about stalls and spins. Many flight instructors have only experienced one anxious half-turn spin when working toward their instructor certificate, and the CFI's apprehension toward spins will forever after be communicated as a danger signal when teaching stalls. An instructor's mental attitude is always picked up by students, usually subliminally.

For that reason, I give students enough time after each stall or spin in this lesson to recuperate with a bit of straight and level flight, perhaps pointing out some landmark ahead in the distance. If the student is suddenly quiet, or doesn't seem on top of control input needs, I can be pretty sure the student's cognitive resources have been overly taxed.

Some aerobatic CFIs save spin instruction for later in their syllabus, but I've found that introducing a recovery from an incipient spin early serves three important objectives:

1. It helps ease any lingering apprehensions about spins.
2. The student experiences how predictable and easy recovery is with the proper sequence of control inputs.
3. It prepares students to recover from an inadvertent spin when they practice solo or take a friend along, which they might do even if you've cautioned against solo practice until they receive spin training. I've had many students put us into a stall on the backside of a loop, or other high G, low speed maneuver, and without some stall practice and spin introduction, they'll often just hold the stick back, dumbfounded by why the nose won't come up.

Lesson 4 – Expanding What You've Learned

Cloverleaf, Inverted Flight, Sustained Stall, Full Turn Spin

Objectives of this lesson

1. Combine two already-learned aerobatic skills into a new, more complex maneuver (cloverleaf).
2. Maintain straight and level flight while inverted.
3. Overcome the airplane's tendency to spin during a sustained stall.
4. Recover from a developed spin.

This lesson will introduce you to a complex maneuver called a cloverleaf, which simultaneously combines a loop and a roll, two maneuvers you have already learned. Performing this complex (but not complicated) maneuver will strengthen your spatial orientation skills and your stick-and-rudder skills, and will increase your use of outside visual references to make your maneuvers precise.

When learning a new aerobatic maneuver, things seem to happen fast at first, but with just a little practice, your perceptions will speed up, making even the most complex aerobatic maneuver seem to slow down.

This lesson also gives you an opportunity to experience a brief amount of inverted flight, which will prepare you for some upcoming maneuvers where you'll experience -1 G (i.e., hanging upside down in your seatbelt). At first, it will feel weird, but try to remember the fun you had as a kid hanging upside down from a tree branch or from playground equipment.

Note: The inverted flight portion of this lesson will be eliminated if your aircraft does not have an inverted fuel and oil system.

You will also practice a spin that's more developed than the one in the last lesson. There are four stages to a spin: **entry, incipient (beginning), developed, and recovery**. A full turn starts the developed stage.

Review

Dutch roll warmup (optional).

Combine a loop ending with an immediate aileron roll to the right (If you've been rolling mostly to the left).

1. Cloverleaf

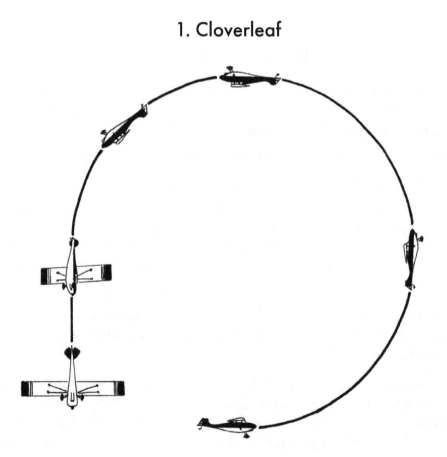

If you like looping and rolling, you'll love the cloverleaf. The above maneuver review suggestion has you flying a loop *and* a roll, but sequencing one at a time. In the cloverleaf, however, you'll be flying a loop *with* a roll. Instead of one maneuver at a time, you'll perform two maneuvers at the same time. Flying the cloverleaf feels like multi-tasking at first, but it gets easier and more fun each time you fly one.

The clover leaf is a quarter-turn roll on the back side of a loop. That will put your exit heading 90° from your entry heading. If you repeated this maneuver three times in a row, you'd have a three-leaf clover. Four times gives you a lucky four-leaf clover, which would return you to your entry heading. In this lesson, you'll perform a one-leaf cloverleaf.

How it's done, where to look

1. Choose an entry reference point on the horizon. If you're flying in an area with straight roads, enter the same direction as one of them to give you an added reference during the quarter-turn rollout on the backside. Otherwise, simply estimate a quarter-turn while glancing at the ground during the third quarter of the loop.

2. Enter a loop. The first half of the loop will be the same as the other loops you have practiced.

3. When your aircraft's nose starts coming down over the top on the third quarter of the loop, start your roll. Continue adding back pressure on the stick, though, because you are still looping while rolling.

4. Keep adding back pressure, but stop your roll after you've made a quarter turn. Look up to find an exit point on the horizon. If you keep looking down, there will be a tendency to stop the back pressure during the roll. Look for an exit point on the horizon that's 90° from your entry heading. Keep pulling on the stick until you are straight and level again, like with any loop.

5. After recovering from the loop, you should be at your beginning altitude, but at a heading of 90° from your entry direction.

Common errors and corrections

- **Relaxing backpressure instead of increasing it during the downline** is the most common error during a cloverleaf. Instead of doing one thing at a time, you'll have to keep pulling back on the stick *while* you are making your quarter-turn roll. Without continuing to pull the nose up, you'll develop excessive speed with an excessive altitude loss, and you'll need to pull more Gs to recover. As soon as your aircraft's nose starts downward in the third quarter of the loop, glance at the reference point that's 90° from your entry reference point and start your combined roll and pullup toward that exit point. As with all loops, you will feel a heavier G-load during the fourth quarter, roughly equal to the way you felt during the first quarter of the loop.

- **The ending heading was not 90° from the entry heading**. You likely over-rolled or under-rolled during the recovery. Watching for your exit reference point is the key to judging the right amount of rollout. Look for your exit reference point during the backside of the loop and your basic flying skills will make the airplane go there. If you fix your gaze straight down, you'll likely head in that direction too long because your subconscious autopilot tends to make the airplane go where you are looking.

2. Inverted Flight

The first time a pilot rolled inverted and back to upright again was September 1, 1913, in a 50 hp Gnome engine Bleriot XI flown by Adolphe Pegöud. The airplane's designer, Louis Bleriot, had fitted the cockpit with belts and straps to keep Pegöud from falling out of the open cockpit. Pegöud took off from the airfield at Juvisy, France, with a crowd of spectators wondering what fantastic feat this famous aerobatic pilot would be demonstrating. At an altitude of about 3,000 feet, Pegöud rolled to the left, and continued rolling until the wheels were straight up. The crowd hushed in horror, but the calm demeaner of Bleriot, who was standing with the spectators, assured everyone that the maneuver was intentional and under control by Pegöud. After about a minute, Pegöud half-rolled to upright, did a few victorious wing-overs, and landed (albeit, drenched in leaked gasoline) to be welcomed by the rush of onlookers.

Special inverted designs

In order to sustain inverted flight, the airplane must have an inverted fuel system and the engine must be designed to bathe the interior moving parts with an inverted oil system. It also helps if the aircraft's wing is designed to be somewhat stable when inverted, which means little, if any, dihedral. A somewhat convex underside of the wing will add lift when inverted. Other common aerobatic airplane features are double seatbelts, with one of them extra wide for comfort and a rachet to tighten your anatomy firmly into the seat. The most important feature to successful inverted flight, however, is a pilot like you who has learned how to control and maneuver the airplane in that attitude.

Pushing on the stick

If you are new to inverted flying, you'll be pleased to know that it's relatively easy to learn, and the calmer you allow yourself to be, the easier it will seem. All the better if you can think of it as fun—because it *is* fun. When you were a kid, you probably loved how it felt when you hung upside down from playground equipment, marveling at how the world looked from that perspective. I mentioned this earlier, but I'm repeating it because so many of my aerobatic students have been told by someone that when flying inverted, it will take tremendous physical strength to push and hold the stick forward enough to keep the nose "up" (toward your feet), and for that reason, you should run the trim all the way forward to help with this super-human task. Don't worry, it doesn't take a lot of muscle to push the stick forward to sustain inverted flight. It might feel strange, though, because if you've never flown upside down before, you've never had a reason to push and hold the control stick forward of neutral during a flight, except for spin recoveries.

Another new experience will be the amount of forward stick travel you'll need to hold the nose up. That's because the horizontal stabilizer on your airplane's tail is designed to produce enough negative lift during right-side up flying in order to hold the nose up at cruise airspeed. In short, it pushes the tail down to hold the nose up. That's why it's called a stabilizer. That stabilizing design makes the nose drop to regain and maintain airspeed whenever the speed gets lower than cruise. When the tail is upside down, however, the horizontal stabilizer continues to produce lift in the same direction relative to the airplane, but now that direction is toward the sky. Simply put, the inverted tail wants to rise up and tilt the nose down toward the earth. You will overcome that inverted tail lift by pushing the stick forward farther than you might expect, but not harder.

Control orientation while inverted

Thinking through how your control inputs have an opposite effect when inverted can seem confusing. I get confused trying to write about it. But you'll be surprised how intuitively you'll fly if you watch the horizon as your guide. It also might help to remember that, regardless of your attitude, you always push the nose toward your feet with forward stick, and you always pull the nose toward your head with backpressure.

During this lesson, you won't be doing anything more challenging than sustaining straight and level inverted flight for a few seconds. One of the main objectives is to get a sight picture of the distance between the horizon and the airplane's nose while maintaining altitude. When you have that picture embedded in your mind, you'll be able to roll in and out of inverted flight with fewer adjustments and greater ease. Another objective of this lesson is to have some fun hanging upside down.

How it's done, where to look

1. Begin with an aileron roll the same way you have been doing, only start adding forward pressure as you roll past knife edge into inverted flight.

2. When inverted, stop rolling, and continue pushing the stick enough to keep the nose above the horizon. Neutralize your rudders.

3. **Glance at your altimeter**. If you are losing altitude, push a bit more. If you are gaining altitude, push a bit less. (No pulling necessary.) Make changes a little at a time. If you feel a sense of urgency, it's from being a little anxious about this strange new aviation experience.

4. When you've stabilized with a constant altitude, notice the distance between the nose and the horizon. **Memorize that sight picture for future reference**. You'll see the world like this during other aerobatic maneuvers.

5. Roll to upright, easing off forward stick pressure as you pass back through knife edge.

Common errors and corrections

- **Inverted dive**. Correct this by pushing on the stick. If the dive seems steep, keep the stick forward while rolling out from inverted, and then recover from the upright dive. **You recover from an inverted dive with a combination of "push-and-roll." Do not** try to pull the nose through as if you were coming off the top of a loop. That's called a split-S, and your already-fast airspeed will accelerate rapidly, you'll lose a lot of altitude, and you'll have to pull an uncomfortably high G-load to recover. (By the way, an intentional split-S starts inverted, but the airspeed is reduced to the edge of minimum controllable airspeed before pulling back on the stick.)

- **Inverted climb**. Ease off forward stick pressure just a little, check your altitude, and then correct a little more if needed. Don't "pull" the stick back because the nose will abruptly drop earthward. Just ease off the forward pressure a little at a time.

- **A wing is lower than the other wing**. Simply roll in the opposite direction until both wings are equidistant from the horizon. Later when you practice turning while inverted, you'll find the airplane will turn in the opposite direction of the aileron control input. The simple explanation is that the wing's lift is reversed, so the control inputs have an opposite effect. We'll discuss more about opposite inverted control effects in a later lesson.

3. One-Turn Spin

Spin signatures

If you still feel adventurous at this point in your flight, a good way to complete the lesson is to perform a spin that develops past the insipient (beginning) stage. Every airplane make and model has its own spin signature, but many aerobatic airplanes will increase their spinning rate during the first few turns, but then centrifugal force brings the nose up enough to stabilize the rate of spin. To see the effect of centrifugal force on a spinning object, tie something like a key onto the end of an eight inch or so piece of string. Hold the other end of the string and twirl the key around. You'll see that the faster you spin the key, the higher it will rise.

Keeping track of rotations

Spatial orientation can be challenging when the spin rate increases. The best way to keep track of where you are is to count revolutions out loud by halves like this: "*Half...one... one-and-a half... two,*" etc. It also helps to keep track of your half-points by spinning over a straight, railroad, or agricultural fence line. If you can't find a nearby straight line, then during your clearing turn chose something prominent on the ground at your initial reference point and another ground reference at the 180° point.

If you ever lose count of your rotations during a spin, recover immediately, or glance at your altimeter and recover at a pre-decided altitude. I've seen confused students stare in awe at the blurry spinning earth, forgetting that it is quickly rushing toward us.

It's not rolling

You are not in a rolling dive during a spin, you are yawing in autorotation during a sustained stall, with one wing stalled more than the other wing. Because you are yawing and not rolling, adding aileron in the opposite direction will NOT help you recover, and, indeed, could aggravate the spin and adversely affect recovery.

How it's done, where to look

1. With power at idle, keep pulling the stick back to maintain altitude.
2. At the first indication of a stall, push one of the rudders fully and pull the stick straight back all the way. Some pilots (including me) use both hands on the stick to help keep the ailerons neutral.

3. At the 180° point, say aloud "Half."

4. At the 270° point, push full opposite rudder, and then push the stick to, or a bit past, neutral. (The Super Decathlon and Aerobat, as examples, need at least a quarter-turn lead to recover from a one-turn spin. Your instructor will tell you the best recovery initiation point for the aircraft you are flying.)

5. When your airspeed starts to increase, pull out of the dive while adding cruise power. Pull with the just-right Goldilocks method: not too hard (to avoid a secondary stall) and not too soft (to minimize altitude loss).

6. Did you exit at your entry heading? How much altitude did you lose?

Common errors and corrections

- **Adding aileron**. The ailerons must be neutral in a spin, otherwise they could adversely affect the recovery. Right-handed pilots sometimes inadvertently pull the stick back and to the right instead of straight back, with the opposite result for lefties. It's helpful to have both hands on the stick to keep it centered while pulling back.

- **Loosing track of rotations and direction**. If you count your spin half-turns aloud, you'll stay spatially oriented. If you get confused about how many turns you've made, recover from the spin immediately.

- **Recovering past the entry heading.** The likely culprit is initiating the recovery too late. Another recovery flub is too little opposite rudder to stop rotation, and/or not enough brisk forward stick to break the stall.

- **The nose comes up and the spin doesn't recover**. If the nose comes up and you see the horizon rapidly rotating by you when you look out the windshield, and the controls are ineffective, then you are likely in a flat spin. The culprit is almost certainly because the engine power is holding the nose up, which is often the case with inadvertent spins. (That's why reducing the power to idle is *always* the first step in the PARE spin recovery method.) If that's the case, reduce the power to idle and the nose will drop down into a normal spin. From that point, recover like you would from any spin. The other possible cause is too much weight too far aft. If that's the problem, the only solution is to move excess weight forward. I don't mean to be flippant, but how you do that while flying the airplane is a problem that's beyond the scope of this book. Someone once told me that a pilot recovered from a flat spin by releasing his seat belt and throwing himself over the instrument panel. I don't suggest counting on that technique. I heard another story about an airplane full of skydivers going into a flat spin. The skydivers simply jumped out of the airplane—weight and balance problem solved. Hint: remember that you are wearing a parachute. Pre-decide on your personal emergency loss-of-control (LOC) bailout altitude, because during an emergency you won't have the time or mental wherewithal to sort it out. Prevention is better than the cure, however, so always perform a weight and balance calculation before every flight.

How Spirals Differs from Spins

There are two types of spirals: a gliding spiral and a diving spiral.

Gliding spirals are useful when you want to lose altitude over something on the ground, such as an airport or other landing spot. It can be used for engine-out landings. You maintain your position over the ground by shallowing your bank on the upwind side of your circle and steepening your bank on the downwind side.

You can control your airspeed and turn rate during a gliding spiral, but as you steepen your bank and lower your nose, vertical lift gives way horizontal lift and gravity takes control of your airspeed. Pulling harder on the stick only tightens the turn. Because of these characteristics, a diving spiral and is considered a loss of control (LOC).

A spiral dive isn't a spin, but it can evolve from one. In a spin, the airplane is yawing while in a sustained nose-down auto-rotational stall. If the airplane recovers from the stall on its own while you are still rotating, it could continue diving in an ever-tightening bank when you continue holding backpressure on the stick. It might look to you like you're still spinning, but in a spiral dive, you'll be pulling centrifugal force Gs because you are in a steep bank. The airspeed will increase rapidly, so glance at the airspeed indicator if you're spinning more than one turn. If you are in a completely stalled spin, the airspeed in most airplanes will rise a little above published stall speed and stay there. If you are spiraling, the airspeed needle will quickly head for the red line, and it's time to recover.

Recovering from a spiral

To recover from a spiral, reduce backpressure on the stick, and roll out with aileron and coordinated rudder inputs, and then carefully pull out of the resulting dive. Don't abruptly yank the ailerons out of the spiraling roll because that could put a tremendous twisting force on the airframe. If you ever see wrinkles on an airplane's fuselage or wings during your pre-flight inspection, the damage could have been caused by someone who flew into a spiral and aggressively yanked out of it. Needless to say, that damage would take the airplane out of service until a licensed mechanic inspected it.

Lesson 5 – Combining Maneuvers
Barrel Roll, Inverted Climbs-Glides-Turns

The objectives of this lesson

1. Merging two primary maneuvers (loop and roll) to form a complex maneuver (barrel roll).
2. Sustaining inverted flight while performing basic maneuvers of climb, glide, dive, and straight and level.

Barrel roll intro

As with the cloverleaf, you'll be merging two basic aerobatic maneuvers you've already learned—a loop and a roll—into an entirely new maneuver called the barrel roll. The barrel roll is more difficult than the cloverleaf, however, because instead of flying with a clear sight of ground references, you will be traveling horizontally, which makes it difficult to keep track of reference ground points. For this reason, the barrel roll is an excellent exercise for your spatial orientation skills, which you'll find handy when you get to more complex maneuvers like the hammerhead, Immelmann, slow roll, snap roll, and avalanche.

Maneuvering while inverted intro

In the second maneuver, you'll be controlling the airplane through the fundamentals of flight—straight and level, turns, climbs, and dives—while inverted. This will give you an opportunity to experience how your control inputs will have an opposite effect when flying inverted. Those skills will help you later master the aforementioned more complex maneuvers, plus the 4-point roll, and split-S. Your inverted flight skills will also be priceless if you ever get flipped upside down from surprises like a strong downdraft or wake turbulence. We'll focus more on extreme attitude surprises in the lesson about upset recoveries.

1. Barrel Roll

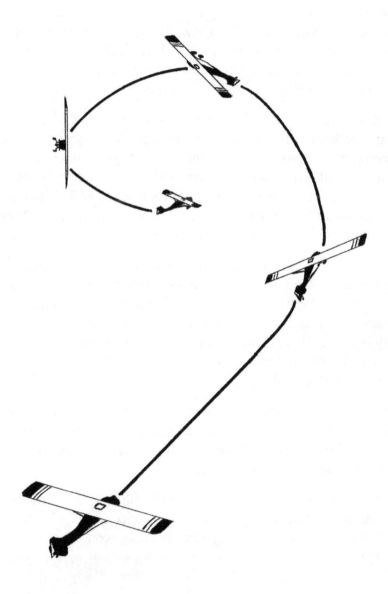

The history of the barrel roll goes back to the early 1900s, but it was not the standard maneuver we know today. Instead, it was usually the start of a loop with random rollouts at various points, looking to both pilot and spectators like graceful soaring and dipping through the sky. For instance, what we know as the cloverleaf today, might have been considered a barrel roll back then. The snap roll (also known as the flick roll) was also called a barrel roll in the early days. But in the 1939 Royal British Air Force Training Manual, a barrel roll was officially defined as a loop and a roll simultaneously blended into one coordinated maneuver. Not a loop and not a roll, but both at the same time. The described maneuver pulls very few Gs, which made some diehard aerobatic aviators smugly consider it a maneuver for pilots who could not tolerate high G loads. But bravado aside, it has become popular with pilots and spectators alike for its grace and precision. Add smoke at an airshow performance, and you get a spectacular corkscrew through the sky.

As I mentioned, the barrel roll pulls a minimum amount of Gs. Even though you are basically flying a corkscrew pattern, it won't look at all like that from the cockpit. It is considered a complex maneuver because you will be flying two maneuvers at the same time, merging a loop with a roll. In other words—and perhaps to complicate things—you'll be rolling throughout the loop while looping throughout the roll. The two challenges are: 1) timing the loop and roll so they start and end at the same time, and 2) keeping track of where you are within the 3D pattern you are making.

Your reference points will also be different than for the preceding maneuvers. You'll be rolling around a point on the horizon that will be offset 45° from your entry heading. But that point will be hard to keep track of, so the reference that you should rely on is making sure your airplane's nose comes down through the horizon while inverted at a point 90° from your entry heading. This is a difficult maneuver to explain or diagram because of its complex pattern, and because it looks very different from the ground than it does from the cockpit (so does the lazy 8, by the way).

Timing your roll with your loop takes practice, as does coordinating them so you are exactly inverted at the 90° point. Ending exactly at the entry point and entry altitude also takes practice. It's a fun and relatively comfortable maneuver, though, so you won't mind practicing until you make it all come together.

This is one maneuver I always show on the ground with a toy airplane, and then I always demonstrate flying one before letting my student practice it. I do that because it looks so different from inside the cockpit than from outside the cockpit.

How it's done, where to look

1. Choose a starting reference point on the horizon, and choose another point 90° in the direction you plan to roll. As always, the entry speed should be according to the aircraft's POH, but it's usually the same as the entry speed for rolls. Notice your starting altitude.

2. Pull up as if entering a loop while starting a gradual roll. The roll needs to be more gradual than the loop because the airplane can complete a roll faster than it can a loop. If you roll out too fast, you'll recover before reaching your entry point. Look for your 90° point as soon as you can see it. Keeping track of that point will help you coordinate your roll with your loop.

3. You are looping, so, like with all loops, pull hard on the first quarter, relax some back pressure while you float over the top, start pulling on the downside, and pull harder on the last quarter. But you are also rolling at the same time. Time your roll so your wings are level and inverted as your nose drops down through the horizon 90° from your entry heading. Keep rolling so you end with wings level and right-side up at your starting point. You should be at the altitude and heading with which you entered the maneuver.

Common errors and corrections

- **Not ending at the starting point.** This could be because you either rolled out too soon, which would make you end the maneuver before reaching your entry point, or you rolled out too late, which will make you end the maneuver past the entry point. It's hard to keep track of your roll rate because you are looping at the same time. Try thinking of it as more of a looping maneuver than a rolling maneuver. The loop sets the pace.

- **Not ending at the starting altitude**. The common reasons are similar to loop errors: not pulling hard enough on the first and last quarters of the loop, or relaxing back pressure too little or too much over the top. Keeping track of where you are in the looping portion of the barrel roll is difficult because you are rolling at the same time. This will get easier to judge with some practice.

2. Inverted Climbs, Glides, and Turns

(This maneuver will be skipped if your airplane does not have an inverted fuel and oil system.)

You will soon be learning maneuvers where you will be inverted part of the time (i.e., Immelmann, Cuban 8, slow roll, split-S), and this exercise will help you be more in control when you are upside-down during those maneuvers.

As you now know, during sustained inverted flight, you hang by your seatbelt. The bottom of the wing becomes the top of the wing, so to speak, so when you bank the airplane, the aileron that would normally be "up" (toward the sky) is now "down" (toward the earth). Because of that reversal, you will use the opposite rudder when initiating a bank, to trim for adverse yaw.

If this seems about as clear as ground fog, don't worry. You'll be making such shallow banks, climbs, and dives in this exercise, nothing alarming will happen if you forget which rudder peddle to push, or even forget about the rudders altogether. You will need coordinated rudder, however, when you roll inverted. When you recover to right-side-up, you'll initiate the roll with opposite rudder, and switch to coordinated rudder when you roll past knife edge to upright. (I use the term "coordinated rudder" as a shortcut for rudder input on the same side as the stick input. When you use opposite rudder to initiate a roll while inverted, however, that is also a coordinated roll.)

This is one of those rare occasions when actually doing something will be easier than just reading about it. You already have intuitive stick and rudder skills, and they will serve you well. If at any time you get confused or uncomfortable, simply roll back to right-side up and take a break. When you perform this exercise in subsequent training flights, it will magically seem easier.

How it's done, where to look

1. Choose a reference point on the horizon. Make a coordinated aileron roll and stop inverted. Find the inverted sight picture you saw through your windshield in a preceding lesson.

2. Glance at your altimeter and adjust your stick pressure for level flight. You already know that it will seem unnatural to push the stick far enough to maintain altitude. Glance at your wingtips and, if necessary, use your ailerons to make them equidistant from the horizon. (Your ailerons will rotate your airplane in the same direction as if you are right-side up, just like when you perform rolls.)

3. After you have stabilized in straight and level inverted flight, push the nose up from the horizon a just few more degrees. After you establish a shallow climb, slowly return to level inverted flight.

4. After you have re-stabilized, ease off on forward stick pressure a little to gently

lower the nose a just few degrees below the horizon. After you establish a shallow dive, push back to level inverted flight.

5. After you have re-stabilized, roll the airplane into a very shallow bank and hold it there. Notice that the airplane rolls the same direction as if you were right-side up, but it will turn in the direction opposite of your stick input. After you've established a turn, roll back to level, and then turn in the opposite direction for a few seconds, and then return to level inverted flight.

6. Roll back to right-side up with a touch of opposite rudder to initiate it. Maintain forward pressure until you pass through knife edge flight, and then switch to coordinated rudder while you pull back on the stick.

Common errors and corrections

- **Losing altitude**. As mentioned previously, the wings of many aerobatic airplanes are designed to sustain inverted flight pretty well, but not as effectively as they do for normal flight. For that reason, you'll have an increased angle of attack. Also, the horizontal stabilizer will be trying to push the tail toward the sky while inverted, which points the nose toward the ground. Pushing the stick far enough forward to overcome both of those factors won't take a lot of muscle power, but it might take some determination.

- **Abandoning inverted flight with a split-S**. A pilot's brain has been conditioned to pull back on the stick to go up, away from the ground. I believe that's why pilots not trained in inverted flight often try to split-S out of an unintended inverted dive. Another factor is that you have learned how to fly loops by now, and with a loop you go from inverted to right-side up by *pulling* on the stick. Those factors can influence a pilot to instinctively recover from inverted flight by pulling back on the stick. Instead, you should abandon the maneuver by pushing on the stick while rolling right-side up—and then pull out of your dive. Keep *"push-and-roll"* as your mantra because a split-S could exceed the airplane's never exceed airspeed, lose a dangerous amount of altitude, result in an accelerated stall, over-stress the airplane, and over-stress you. Later in this course you'll learn intentional split-Ss, which are fun, and you'll practice inverted dive recoveries later in the Upset Prevention and Recovery" lesson, but for now memorize *Push-and-roll, Push-and-roll, Push-and-roll* if you find yourself in an inverted dive.

At the beginning of this book, I mentioned getting caught in wake turbulence, and a mountain downdraft, and recovering within two or three seconds. I told you about the mountain downdraft incident, and now I'll tell you about the wake turbulence ordeal.

Several years ago, I was flying a Cessna 172 with a non-pilot friend into the Minneapolis-St. Paul International Airport (when GA aircraft commonly landed there). I was following a heavy, slow Air Force C-130 on final, and the tower cautioned me about possible wake turbulence. I was a mile or so behind the C-130, and there was a slight crosswind, which I thought would drift the C-130's vortexes out of the way in time. It did, but not enough. When I was on a short final, the wake caught one wing and flipped us past knife edge—and *that's* inverted. As you now know, if you pull back on the stick anytime past knife edge, you dive toward the ground. Because I was trained in aerobatics, I automatically and immediately pushed and rolled back to normal flight attitude, and made a very nice landing. My friend, however, didn't think there was anything nice about it.

Now you have a better understanding of why I'm so passionate about pilots getting basic aerobatic training. I hope you'll acquire the same opinion and share it with other pilots when you experience how the skills you've learned throughout this curriculum come together in the later section on extreme attitude upset recoveries.

Lesson 6 – Increasing Spatial Orientation

Immelmann, Sustained Stall, Humpty Bump, 1 ½-Turn Spin

The objectives of this lesson

1. Combine two half-maneuvers (half-loop, half-roll) into a new aerobatic maneuver (Immelmann).
2. Experience the flight characteristic and spin tendencies during a sustained stall.
3. Maintain spatial orientation and anticipate recovery lead time when the number of spin rotations fully develop.

1. Immelmann

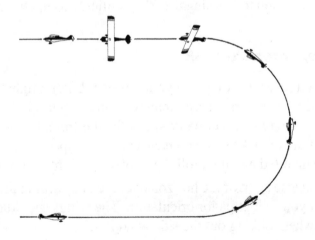

World War I German ace Max Immelmann made famous what was then called the *looping helicoidal*, a maneuver we now call the Chandelle. He used it as a tactical maneuver, firing on his enemy from behind, and then maximized his airplane's momentum energy and engine power to climb as high as possible without stalling, while turning 180°. His resulting direction and higher altitude made it very difficult for the enemy pilot to return fire, even if the pilot was still alive and not busy fighting flames. Immelmann gradually steepened his bank angle, sacrificing some climb energy for a quicker turn-around, and renamed the maneuver the Immelmann Turn. Thanks to the advent of ailerons replacing wing warping, and more powerful engines, the maneuver evolved into a half-loop with a rollout on top. It's now commonly just called the Immelmann because the change of direction results from a half-loop instead of a climbing turn.

The barrel roll gave you experience in blending two fundamental aerobatic maneuvers, loop and roll, into an entirely new maneuver. In flying the Immelmann, you'll also use your looping and rolling skills, but not simultaneously. You will be flying half of a loop, pause inverted, and make a half-roll to return right-side up. During that momentary pause on top you'll use your new inverted flying skills to maintain altitude and initiate the rollout with a touch of opposite rudder.

Another version of the Immelmann is entering the half-loop, then begin the rollout as soon as the nose begins to go inverted, timing the rollout so you'll be inverted exactly at your 180° point. That is a more fluid version, and is the one used in aerobatic competition. In competition, the version described in this lesson would be considered two maneuvers (a half-loop followed by a half-roll), but it more directly relates to the two-point roll skills you just learned in the last lesson. This two-part maneuver is sometimes called the "military version," and the more fluid type is called "competition version." Mastering the military version is a good first step to learning the more difficult competition version.

How it's done, where to look

1. Notice your entry heading and your altitude. Enter a tight loop with slightly more G-force during the first quarter than with ordinary loops. Your airplane POH might also recommend a higher entry speed for the Immelmann than for a loop. These measures are to make sure you have enough airspeed remaining on top of the loop to pause inverted and then roll the airplane upright without stalling.

2. When you lose sight of the horizon over the nose during the beginning of the loop, glance at your wingtips for orientation. The wings should be equidistant from the horizon when looking out the side windows.

3. When you begin flying inverted, look out the windshield for your memorized

inverted flight sight picture. Push on the stick to stop the loop in that attitude, and then roll upright. Your exit heading should be 180° from your entry heading. Notice how much altitude you gained. That's about how much altitude you gain at the apogee (highest point) of a loop.

Common errors and corrections

- **Ending in a dive after rolling right-side up.** If your nose is lower than for normal level flight after rolling upright, you probably had insufficient forward stick pressure when you paused inverted, and/or let off on the forward pressure before you reached knife edge on your rollout. Another common reason for the resulting dive is that you might not have started adding backpressure after passing through knife edge when rolling right-side up.

- **Ending in a direction other than 180° from your entry point.** This could be because you let a wing drop somewhere in the half-loop. Glancing at your wingtips while inverted will remind you to correct any bank you have. Another possible reason is that you didn't use appropriate, or sufficient, rudder to coordinate your rollout. An uncoordinated rollout will result in the airplane yawing away from 180° rollout point. When you begin the rollout from inverted, you might need a touch of opposite rudder to compensate for adverse yaw, especially if your airplane has a short fuselage (less leverage, more yaw potential). When you roll out past knife-edge, you'll be returning to right-side up, and will use the rudder on the same side as your stick pressure to coordinate the roll.

- **While inverted, the airplane stalls.** If the airplane goes into an outside stall while flying inverted, you likely either didn't have enough airspeed on top, or you pushed too abruptly on the stick when entering inverted flight—or both. At the first sign of an outside stall (i.e., burbling airflow, a wing drops), ease off on your forward stick pressure to lower the nose into a shallow airspeed-gaining inverted dive, and then roll upright.

- **The airplane went into an outside spin.** Because the airspeed is relatively low on top of the loop, you might have pushed too hard on the stick to pause inverted, or you paused too long, or both. This situation is ripe for an unintended inverted stall that can quickly evolve into an outside spin. Your instructor will likely need to take over the controls if this happens. This is why you should not practice Immelmanns (or hammerhead turns) solo without first learning how to competently recover from inverted stalls and outside spins. I include inverted stall and spin recognition and recovery in a later lesson.

2. Sustained Stall

Keeping the airplane upright while stalled is more of an upset recognition exercise than an aerobatic maneuver, but in case you inadvertently pinch a maneuver (accidentally exceed critical angle of attack), you'll appreciate having advanced stall skills. You'll experience how the airplane fights against the stall, trying to recover, while the nose yaws back and forth trying to enter a spin. This exercise will give you some valuable critical angle of attack awareness and recovery practice.

Tap dancing on the rudders

When one wing catches a bit more air than the other one, it will lift and yaw the nose in the opposite direction. When that happens, you'll have to quickly use opposite rudder to prevent that yaw from developing into a spin. If you push the rudder too long, the other wing will lift and you'll have to quickly push the other rudder. Doing this exercise with most airplanes will keep your rudder feet very busy. The trick is to add just enough rudder just long enough to prevent a spin. If you over-control, your feet will have trouble keeping up with the airplane's instability.

Keep your ailerons neutral throughout this practice. You want to get used to correct yawing problems with rudders. When you are stalled, ailerons can exacerbate spin tendencies.

New recovery and valuable awareness

This exercise is intended to make you forever aware of what a stall and an imminent spin feels like. It will help you recognize the danger of flying at a low altitude, with a high angle of attack, low airspeed, perhaps cross-controlling. That's the recipe for a stall that pops immediately into a spin.

How it's done, where to look

1. Enter an idle-power stall, with the *ailerons remaining neutral* throughout the maneuver. Note your entry altitude.
2. Hold the stick fully back and correct any yawing or wing lifting with opposite rudder. (NOT ailerons.)
3. If the stall progresses to a spin, recover to normal flight.
4. After a few seconds, recover from the stall. Note your exit altitude.

Common errors and corrections

- **The airplane yaws back and forth too rapidly to correct**. If you feel like you're constantly pushing back and forth on the rudder pedals to prevent a spin, you might not be adding opposite rudder soon enough, maybe holding that rudder too long, or you might be over-correcting with too much opposite rudder.

- **The airplane yawed into a spin**. You might have corrected with the opposite rudder too late, too little, or held it too long. At some point, the yaw can pack enough swing to make the spin unavoidable. In that case, recover from the spin and resume normal flight.

- **The airplane wouldn't stay stalled**. Maybe you didn't have the stick fully back, or maybe your airplane make/model is designed to strongly resist stalling. Airplanes that are designed specifically and uncompromisingly for aerobatics, however, will usually stall crisply, immediately, and stay stalled as long as you want them to.

3 – Humpty Bump

The humpty bump is a vertical upline, a half loop on top, and a vertical line back down. It sounds simple, but there are a few challenges. First, the half-loop on top must be of equal radius throughout the arc. Because you will be entering the half-loop from an airspeed-reducing vertical upline, you'll need to use enough backpressure to overcome sluggish elevator response. After the nose floats over the top, you'll need to ease off the backpressure to keep the half-loop's radius consistent.

Another challenge will be overcoming yaw tendencies because of gyroscopic forces from the prop. You might need right rudder on the slow upline. As you pick up speed on the downline, you might need left rudder (in an American airplane) to overcome yaw.

The third challenge will be keeping your upline and downline exactly vertical. If you glance at your wingtips, they should be equidistant and perpendicular to the horizon. (As always in this book, I assume your aerobatic training airplane does not have a sighting device. Even if it does, you should get used to orienting yourself without a sighting device, in case you later fly an aerobatic airplane that doesn't have one.)

"Humpties," as they're sometime nicknamed, are an excellent spatial orientation exercise, and they're a lot of fun. Here's the drill…

How it's done, where to look

1. Establish the entry speed you'd use for an Immelmann. You'll need the extra airspeed on top to round out the half-loop.

2. Pull assertively into an upline. Glance quickly at your wingtips to make sure you are perfectly vertical.

3. As soon as you've established your vertical line, pull into the half-loop. Glancing at your wingtips will help you keep the half-loop round.

4. After making the half-loop on top, establish a perfectly straight vertical downline. Check your wingtips again.

5. As soon as you've established your vertical downline, pull assertively into straight and level horizontal flight.

In summary, fly straight up, loop over the top, dive straight down, pull up to straight-and-level flight.

Common errors and corrections

- **Entry altitude was different than exit altitude**. That's not an error. Your exit altitude will likely be lower because the vertical dive will be faster than the vertical climb.

- **The exit heading was different than entry altitude**. That's likely due to propeller gyroscopic forces and asymmetrical disk loading (P-factor) during, or after completing, your up vertical line and/or downline. Check your wingtips, on the upline and downline, and if they are not equidistant from the horizon, use your rudder to yaw the nose back in line.

- **I couldn't tell if the half-loop was a perfectly symmetrical arc**. You can't determine the half-loop symmetry by just looking out of the windshield. You'll need to spot-check your wingtips to see if they are drawing a nice arc on the horizon.

4. 1½-Turn Spin

You are gradually building toward multi-turn spins. The 1½ spin will give you more practice in maintaining situational awareness and spatial orientation by counting each half turn aloud ("Half…One…One and a half"). You'll also learn that you'll need more recovery lead time when the airplane's spin rate accelerates.

As spins increase their rotation rate, they might look like a blur at first, but it will soon look slower to you. The maneuver doesn't get slower—your brain speeds up and makes it appear slower.

How it's done, where to look

1. Enter an idle-power spin, preferable over a road or some other recognizable feature to keep track of the number of revolutions. Note your entry altitude to compare with your exit altitude.

2. At the first indication of a stall, push one of the rudders fully, and pull the stick all the way straight back. *Keep the ailerons neutral.*

3. At the 180° point, say aloud "Half."

4. At the 360° point, say aloud "One," and begin to recover with opposite rudder, then push the stick forward past neutral. (NOTE: *Never push the stick all the way forward or you could crossover into an outside spin.*)

5. When you've stopped spinning after the final half-turn, neutralize your controls and say aloud "One and a half" and pull out of the dive. (*Always neutralize your controls when the spin stops, or you could start spinning in the other direction.*) Note your altitude loss.

6. Optional: After you and the airplane have recovered to normal flight, climb to your entry altitude again and perform another 1½ turn spin in the opposite direction. You need to practice spins both ways to create a full spin recovery repertoire. If you are not enthused about a repeat performance at this time, save it for the next lesson.

Common errors and corrections

- **Recovering past the exit point**. The likely reason is that you started the recovery too late. Things happen fast as the rotation rate increases. Another possibility is that you didn't use full opposite rudder, or didn't push the stick far enough, or didn't push it in time to break the stall at your recovery point.

- **Recovering before the exit point**. You either started recovering too soon, or your airplane is a fast spin stopper. I've found with the Super Decathlon, for example, that opposite rudder immediately slows the rotation, and then forward stick stops it dead-on. This allows me to nail the exit heading.

- **Not calling out your half-points (Tsk-tsk!)**. You might have lost track during the excitement of the spin, or just forgot. I'm calling this omission an error because saying aloud your half-turn positions is the best way to keep track of your rotations. I've often had students forget to call out their half-turns, and think they made 1½ turns when it was more like 2 or 3 turns with a greater-than-expected altitude loss. *You must train your spatial orientation skills with half-turn callouts during fast-moving, multi-turn spins.*

- **I started spinning in the opposite direction, or I went into an outside spin.** Those errors are very rare. Check out Steps 4 and 5 above to prevent either of these problems, but if they do occur, recover like you would from any other inside or outside spin. But since you likely haven't practiced outside spins yet in your flight training, your flight instructor will gladly (and eagerly!) perform the recovery for you.

Lesson 7 – Recovering from Pinched Maneuvers

Cuban 8, Outside Stall and Spin, Split-S

The objectives of this lesson

1. Learn how a complex aerobatic maneuver (Cuban 8) can be made by combining three already-learned maneuvers: a partial loop, a rollout from an inverted dive, and a 45° downline.

2. Recognize what an inverted stall and outside spin looks and feels like, and learn how to recover with minimum altitude loss.

3. Experience the altitude loss and airspeed gain from performing a low-airspeed split-S.

1. Cuban 8

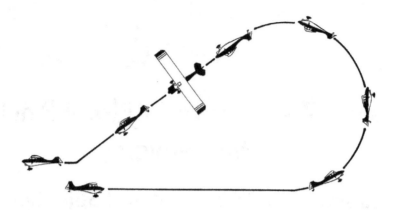

The Cuban 8 was born of a blundered aerobatic maneuver that was recovered imaginatively on the spot. Len Povey was a pilot for the US Army Air Service in the 1930s, and after being discharged, he became an aerobatic competition champion and airshow pilot. As an airshow performer, he specialized in a spectacular night performance, with fireworks attached to his wings spewing glittering sparks across the night sky. One such performance was attended by a scout for Cuban president Batista, who was looking for a great pilot in America to train his Cuban Air Force pilots. After one of Povey's dazzling night airshows, the scout excitedly reported to Batista that he found the greatest pilot in America. Povey agreed to the assignment of training Cuban Air Force pilots, and while living in Havana in 1936, he entered an American aerobatic competition in Florida (only 90 miles from Cuba) with a Cuban Air Force Curtiss Hawk. He planned to do a triple snap roll on the top of a loop, but his airspeed on top of the loop was 140 mph, which was too fast to safely snap roll. Instead, he flew inverted over the top of the loop, and with still too much airspeed for the backside of the loop, he decided to abort the loop with a 45° inverted downline, and then rolled out. It ran through his mind that the maneuver, although botched, probably looked pretty good from the ground, so he pulled into another loop and made the same recovery on the other end, making the entire maneuver look from the ground like a figure 8. After he landed, he was asked by the judges what that spectacular new maneuver was called. He said, "Oh…a…that was a Cuban Figure 8."

In the first lesson of this curriculum, you learned fundamental maneuvers that will now be elements of a more complex maneuver, namely, the Cuban 8. Your stick-and-rudder skills have gradually evolved, as have your spatial orientation skills. If, for example, you would have tried to learn the Cuban 8 on Lesson 1, it would likely have been an incomprehensible, uncoordinated blur that might have discouraged you about aerobatic flying. But now you are ready to bring your acquired aerobatic skills together to perform this graceful, exciting maneuver.

The Cuban 8 starts with a loop that you will abort after rounding the loop's apogee (highest point) by pushing into an inverted dive with a 45° downline. As soon as you establish that downline, roll out and continue diving to reach the entry speed for another loop; then do it all over again. After the second inverted dive, rollout to normal straight and level flight to end the maneuver.

Let's break that down by the numbers.

How it's done, where to look

1. Find an entry reference point on the horizon, and during your clearing turn look for a reference point 180° behind the entry point.

2. Enter a loop with the normal loop entry speed. (Unlike with the Immelmann, you won't need extra airspeed on top of the loop because the nose will be pointed downward during the rollout from inverted.)

3. When your nose begins to drop after rounding the loop's apogee, pick a point about halfway between the horizon and straight down, and push the stick forward enough to dive toward directly at that point on the ground. This will put you into an inverted dive with a 45° downline. (To determine the 45° downline, you could also glance at a wingtip and notice when it is 45° to the horizon. Most students, however, find this harder than the first method.)

4. Immediately after establishing the 45° inverted downline, push the stick forward while rolling upright, and maintain your 45° downline.

5. As soon as you've reached loop entry speed, repeat the maneuver. (As an option when performing this maneuver for the first time, you could exit after the first half of the "8" figure. I usually recommend this to students because the complex attitude and reference point changes can seem a bit much at first.)

6. After performing the second half of the "8," roll out of the inverted dive to a straight-and-level attitude.

Common errors and corrections

- **Not maintaining the 45° downline.** If you had chosen a point on the ground that wasn't exactly 45°, that's fine for now. But if you let your nose rise noticeably (from pushing the stick too much while inverted) or drop too much (not enough forward pressure while inverted or during the rollout), then make corrections with ground reference points. Check your 45° downline again after rolling to upright. Remember, the airplane will tend to go where you are looking, so aim at your 45° point on the ground.

- **Finishing at a heading other than the entry point**. Any time your wingtips are not equidistant from the horizon—while either right-side up or inverted—you will be rolling slight, and probably turning. You'll have time to glance at both wings at the apogee of the loop, and again after rolling out on the 45° downline.

- **Excessive speed on the 45° downline**. You might have pulled into the downline too soon. Ease off your backpressure over the top, like with any loop, before pulling into the 45° downline. Another reason for excess speed is delaying the rollout from inverted, and not starting the second loop soon enough. Start your second loop as soon as you reach the loop entry airspeed.

2. Inverted Stall (aka, Outside Stall)

During this maneuver, you will be recovering at the first indication of the stall. By this time in the curriculum, you have already flown inverted, and you consciously and sub-consciously took in a lot of information during those brief, but valuable, learning experiences. Rolling inverted will seem easier this time, and increasingly easier every time you do it.

Although this maneuver is informally called an "inverted stall," it is actually an outside maneuver because you will be pushing on the stick to stall, which results in a negative critical angle of attack. You will usually be inverted when entering the maneuver, but not necessarily so. You can, in fact, enter an inverted stall while flying right-side up if you push hard enough on the stick while at a low airspeed.

The purpose of this exercise is less about an aerobatic maneuver, and more about upset recovery. You've learned two complex maneuvers—the Immelmann and the Cuban 8—that involved inverted negative-G flying. You know that stalls can happen on purpose or inadvertently with positive or negative critical angles of attack, either upside down or right-side up. This exercise will help you further your stall recovery repertoire.

How it's done, where to look

1. Roll inverted and establish straight and level inverted flight, noticing where the horizon is relative to the top and bottom of the windshield.

2. Bring the power to idle, and maintain your altitude by increasing forward pressure

on the stick. Keep the ailerons and rudders neutral throughout the maneuver.

3. At the first indication of a stall (i.e., wings buffeting or the nose suddenly dips), lower the nose to a shallow inverted dive to recover from the stall.

4. When the airspeed increases, push the nose back up to level inverted flight and add power to cruise.

5. Roll to upright and take a deep breath.

Common errors and corrections

- **Recovering before the stall**. If you are a little anxious, you might think the airplane is stalling when the nose is simply dropping because of decreasing airspeed. Wait until you feel the wing buffeting, but if you are in doubt, go ahead and recover.

- **Lowering the nose too far to recover**. It's easy to let the nose drop too steeply when you recover from the stall because the airplane's design and gravity gremlins are tugging at the nose. If the result is a steep inverted dive, you'll lose more altitude than necessary, and experience heavier negative Gs when you push the nose back up. However, whenever you find yourself in an inverted dive and get flustered about what to do next, remember the magic words: "***Push and roll***." That's short for **pushing the nose to prevent the inverted dive from steepening, while rolling upright, then pulling out of the upright dive**. (You'll continue seeing "push and roll" reminders throughout this curriculum.)

- **A wing is low when you recover**. You might have unintentionally rolled a little during the stall entry, maybe because you didn't keep the stick centered, or the nose might have yawed during the entry, giving rise to one wing. Using both hands on the stick can help keep it forward and in the middle. Another reason for the drooped wing might be the onset of a spin. For this lesson, recover from the stall as indicated above, and level your wings afterward.

3. Inverted Spin (aka Outside Spin)

This is an optional maneuver for this lesson. You might not have time for it, and if the inverted stall was a bit much, tell your instructor that you would like to save the inverted spin for another training flight.

I used the term "inverted spin" for the title of this maneuver because it's a progression from what I had called an "inverted stall" in the prior maneuver. I'm trying to keep the titles clear and consistent, but both the so-called "inverted stall" and the "inverted spin" are very much outside maneuvers. That's because you will be pushing on the stick and stalling with a negative critical angle of attack.

To further this point, you can enter a positive G ("inside") spin while flying inverted by pulling back sufficiently on the stick. For example, if you pull too hard and too soon while slowly rounding the top of a loop, you might feel the wings burble because of a partial stall. You are inverted, but you *pulled* into an inside stall. Centrifugal force was keeping you planted in your seat, and the angle of attack was positive. Let's take a moment to simplify these descriptions.

For simplicity and appropriateness, from now on I'll describe stalls and spins with negative critical angles of attack—from pushing on the stick—as "outside" maneuvers.

During an outside spin with a high-wing aerobatic airplane, the yawing will be more pronounced than during a positive-G inside spin. That's because during an inside spin, you and the engine (the heavy parts) are below the yawing wing, which has a stabilizing effect. It will look to you like you are rotating straight downward, but you are actually yawing with the nose slightly up. During an *outside* spin in a high-wing airplane, however, the wing is below the heavy engine, and centrifugal force is throwing that weight outward— hence, more pronounced and erratic yawing. This yawing differential effect is reduced in bi-wing and mid-fuselage wing airplanes.

To recover from an outside spin, use the same procedure you have been using for inside spins. *

P – Power to idle (although you'll start this exercise with idle power)

A – Ailerons neutralized

R – Rudder pushed fully in the opposite direction of rotation

E – Elevator pulled back (pull back for an outside spin, push forward for an inside spin) a bit past neutral to recover from the stall **

---

* Be sure to consult the airplane manufacturer's POH, and follow their recovery technique if it differs from this one.

** After you recover from the outside spin, bring the airplane back to normal upright by pulling up out of your dive when your airspeed begins to increase, and add power.

How it's done, where to look

1. Enter an inverted idle-powered stall, like in the previous maneuver.

2. When the wings start to stall add full rudder on one side, and full forward pressure on the stick.

3. As soon as the nose drops and begins to rotate, add full opposite rudder and bring the stick back just past neutral (or where recommended by your airplane's POH).

4. As airspeed increases, pull the nose up to right-side up flight with backpressure on the stick while adding cruise power. (As an option, you can push the nose back to inverted flight, but you'll pull some extra negative Gs. A few negative Gs won't hurt you, but they'll feel strange unless you are a trapeze artist.)

Common errors and corrections

- **Letting go of forward pressure too soon**. When the airplane starts to spin, add opposite rudder *first* to slow or stop rotation, and *then* bring the stick back past neutral.

- **Entering a spin in the other direction**. If you delay bringing the stick back to break the stall after applying full opposite rudder, the airplane could start spinning in the other direction. Add your recovery control inputs without delays—full opposite rudder, stick back to recover from the stall.

- **Delaying rudder and control stick inputs**. The erratic yawing might fascinate and distract you from recovering. Focus on your plan: as soon as the nose drops, bring power to idle; ailerons neutral; opposite rudder; stick back past neutral; pull upright out of your dive when airspeed increases.

- **Delaying a pullup after the stall and spin is stopped**. Remember, your goal is to minimize altitude loss from any stall or spin. You can always deliberately override that automatic response if, for example, you planned to immediately enter another maneuver after the spin and need more speed, or for competition, where you are expected to recover with a straight downline before pulling up.

- **Entering an inside spin**. This is a very rare outside spin error, but if you kept the rudder in and pulled the stick all the way back, the airplane could crossover into an inside spin. You would have to be severely confused to make such a control error— or, you might be doing that on purpose because crossover spins are interesting. Save learning deliberate crossovers, however, for an advanced spin course.

4. Split-S

I've talked about the split-S elsewhere in this curriculum as something you should never do if you find yourself in an unintended rollover, an inverted dive, or if you start losing control during inverted flight. That credo still stands. But the split-S can be a legitimate aerobatic maneuver when entered from inverted at a low airspeed. Keep in mind that you'll still lose lots of altitude fast, so begin with an extra altitude safety margin. Your airspeed will also increase quickly, so pull hard enough to shorten your diving time, but not so hard that you exceed the critical angle of attack (AOA) and stall.

How it's done, where to look

1. Note your altitude. Roll inverted and reduce your power to idle.
2. Push on your stick forward enough to maintain altitude.
3. When you first feel evidence of an imminent stall (i.e., fluttering wings, diminished control authority), pull the stick back to recover, as if you were flying through the back half of a loop.
4. As airspeed increases, pull harder to minimize altitude loss, but be careful not to pull too hard or too soon or you might stall. This should be a familiar experience because it's like flying the third and fourth quarters of a loop.
5. As soon as you recover to straight and level, notice your airspeed and altitude loss.

Common errors and corrections

- **Entering a stall or spin during the recovery**. You likely pulled too hard, too soon, or both, and you can stall in any attitude if you exceed critical AOA. Whenever you feel the airplane shuddering from a partial stall, ease off on stick backpressure enough to gain a bit more airspeed, and then resume your pull-back.
- **Gaining too much airspeed during the dive**. If you delay backpressure during the back of a loop, you'll pick up excessive airspeed. Think of a split-S as the back half of a loop.

Lesson 8 – Fine Tuning Stick-and-Rudder Skills

Slow Roll, Reverse Cuban 8, 2-Turn Spin

The objectives of this lesson

1. Roll equidistantly around a point on the horizon, with the ability to stop and resume at any point (slow roll).
2. Maintain control during a maneuver that requires changing stick and rudder inputs, sometimes cross-controlling, throughout the maneuver (slow roll).
3. Rolling inverted on a 45° upline (Cuban 8).
4. Make a precise spin recovery after multiple turns.

1. Slow Roll

"Slow roll" is somewhat of a misnomer because the roll rate can actually be very fast, depending on the airplane and the pilot's intentions. Aerobatic biplanes, for example, can generally roll faster because they have short wings, four ailerons, and plenty of total wing surface. (Using the figure skater again as an example, the spinning skater can increase her spinning rate by bringing her arms in closer to her body, and then slow her spin rate by extending her arms outward.)

On the other hand, the slow roll can be very slow, indeed, even stopping at various points: i.e., two-point, four-point, or eight-point rolls.

The slow roll is different in other ways from the aileron roll that you already learned. For starters, the slow roll will make an equidistant (constant radius) circle around a reference point on the horizon. The aileron roll, however, is more of a half-roll, forming a D-shape instead of an O-shape with the nose.

The big difference, though, is that while an aileron roll requires coordinated stick and rudder inputs all the way around, the slow roll requires shifting from coordinated flight while upright (before passing through knife edge), to adding opposite rudder and forward pressure (uncoordinated flight) while rolling past knife edge, and then back again with coordinated control inputs on the second half. If you are stopping at four points, you will be holding the nose up while at knife edge with the skyward rudder.

If that sounds mind-numbingly complex, you probably know by now that many of these maneuvers are easier to do than to think about, and they get even easier with some practice. Eventually, though, you'll perform complicated maneuvers without thinking through all the steps you are taking. It's like driving a car. You can drive without consciously thinking through all your control inputs, but what would you tell a student driver who asks you how many revolutions of the steering wheel it takes to make a 90° turn? (Flight instructors sometimes get questions of that sort, but we often cop out with something like "That's a good question—let's try it and see.)

The slow roll is one of the most beautiful, graceful-looking aerobatic maneuvers, a staple of airshow pilots, and named the "victory roll" by World War II fighter pilots. For all its exterior grace and beauty, though, it doesn't feel graceful from inside the cockpit, and the constantly changing control inputs will keep you busy. You will also be pushing on the stick throughout most of the roll to prevent turning and to prevent diving while inverted.

Let's sort this out by going through the numbers.

How it's done, where to look

1. **Horizon reference point.** Notice your entry altitude and choose a reference point on the horizon. You'll want your nose to roll a constant-radius circle around this point. Watch your point and trust that your stick and rudder skills will keep the nose equidistant around that point during the entire roll.

2. **Roll.** Make a coordinated roll to one side, pushing enough forward stick to keep the airplane from entering a turn (Dutch rolls prepared you for this).

3. **Knife edge.** As you approach knife edge, start adding opposite "up" rudder to hold the nose up toward the sky. You'll be cross-controlled, and you'll feel gravity tugging your body to one side. The slower the roll, the more awkward this will feel at first. You'll soon learn to enjoy feeling awkward.

4. **Inverted past knife edge.** When you roll past knife edge, you will be flying inverted. Push enough forward stick and enough opposite rudder to keep the nose equidistant from your reference point. Watch your point and your intuitive flying skills will serve you well.

5. **Neutral rudders at the apogee.** When you are inverted at the apogee of the roll, neutralize your rudders, but keep rolling with aileron pressure. As you roll past the apogee, start adding coordinated rudder (same side as your stick pressure) to hold the nose "up" toward the sky. The only thing giving your airplane lift while knife edge on either side of the maneuver is the side of the fuselage. You'll have to supplement that inadequate lift surface with lots of rudder. Also keep forward pressure as needed to keep the airplane from entering a turn or diving through your reference point.

6. When you pass knife edge, start adding enough back pressure to keep the nose equidistant from your point, and hold enough rudder to keep the roll coordinated. When the wings are level, stop the roll. Notice whether your exit altitude is the same as your entry altitude.

Tip: Train your eyes on the horizon reference point, and if your nose is constantly equidistant around that point, you are making a nice slow roll, no matter how clumsy it might feel.

This is a "looks cool" maneuver, not a "feels comfy" maneuver.

Common errors and corrections

- **The nose went through the reference point**. The most common reasons for flying through your point are:
  o Insufficient forward pressure at the beginning of the roll, which allowed the airplane to start turning into the point. You want to roll, but not turn. Remember Dutch rolls.
  o Not adding enough forward pressure while inverted to keep the nose above your point. Remember your inverted sight picture.
  o Not enough opposite rudder to keep the nose up while flying through knife

edge. This will be especially important if you are making a 4-point roll, where you'll pause at knife edge. This takes practice because things are happening fast, most airplanes don't fly very well on their sides, and none of this feels right.

- **Recovering past the reference point**. To prevent the nose from yawing out past the point at the end, use enough coordinated rudder during the last quarter of the roll on the side you are rolling. In other words, if you are pushing the stick to the left, you will be adding left rudder between the final knife edge and completion of the maneuver. This will give you a coordinated rollout without the nose yawing out at the end.

- **Not keeping the nose up while knife edged**. That might be from an insufficient amount of corrective rudder. It could also be from rolling too slowly for the airplane's power and design, or for your present skill level.

- **The whole maneuver was a mess**. That's not uncommon for the first time someone performs a slow roll. It's a complex maneuver with ever-changing control inputs, some of them uncoordinated. That's why it comes this late in the curriculum, after you've had a chance to build all the fundamental skills that come together for a perfect roll. Here are some practice exercises my students have found helpful:

  o **Practice two-point rolls**. Sometimes I introduce students to the slow roll by performing a two-pointer first. That gives you time to stabilize in familiar inverted flight, time to think about what's next, and time to reset your spatial orientation.

  o **Practice stopping at knife edge** but then immediately roll back to upright. This gives you practice with that first quarter of the roll, which needs to be somewhat correct for the rest of the maneuver to work out.

  o **Fly inverted for a few seconds** before starting your slow roll. This can remind your mental muscle memory to push the stick during most of the slow roll. It's like a golfer taking a few practice swings to get the feel of the club.

  o **Practice different roll rates.** The slow roll is easier when the airplane rolls quickly, but you'll develop better skills by rolling slowly. This is why fast-rolling airplanes are not always the best primary aerobatic trainers. Their fast roll rate makes it too easy. The slow roll needs to be studied and perfected with slow execution.

  o **And the most important remedial exercise of all**: keep your eyes glued to the reference point throughout the maneuver. As a certificated pilot, your brain is already wired to use correct control inputs once your eyes tell your brain where your airplane's nose is and where you want it to be. When you make a perfect circle around your point, you are making a perfect slow roll—even if it felt weird and you're not quite sure how you did it.

2. Reverse Cuban 8

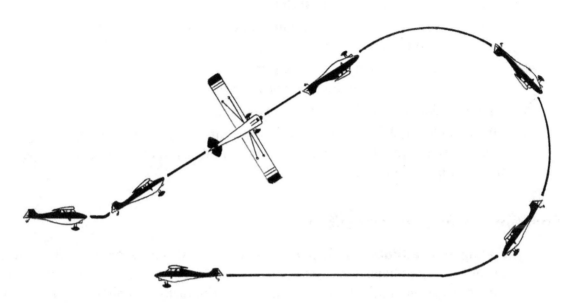

A reverse Cuban 8 makes the same familiar vertical figure 8 in the sky as the regular Cuban 8, but the "reverse" refers to a different entry and exit. Instead of rolling off the back of a loop into a 45° downline, you'll start by pulling up into a 45° upline, rolling inverted, and then entering the second half of a loop from the top. It will be an inside loop because you'll be pulling positive Gs throughout the loop. When you complete the half-loop, you'll reestablish your entry speed, pull up into another 45° upline, and do it all over again.

As with the normal Cuban 8, the completed maneuver won't look like an eight-shape from inside the cockpit, but it will to people watching from the ground. Conversely, the lazy 8 looks like an eight-shape from inside the cockpit, but it just looks like a couple of graceful wing-overs to people watching from the ground. This is probably why you'll see reverse and normal Cuban 8s in airshows, but not lazy 8s. Work through both of the maneuvers on the ground with a toy airplane, and you'll see what I mean.

This maneuver relies on skills you learned earlier in this curriculum: flying 45° lines, loops, inverted flight, and combined and complex maneuvers.

How it's done, where to look

1. It's best to do this over a road to keep your headings in line, or you can pick a reference point on the horizon. Note your entry altitude.

2. Increase your speed a few knots above your aileron roll entry speed. You'll use up the extra airspeed during the next step.

3. Bring the nose up to a 45° upline. Glance at your wingtips to estimate the correct angle in relation to the horizon.

4. When you are at the aileron roll entry speed, roll inverted. Keep enough forward pressure to hold the 45° upline for a brief moment.

5. Bring the stick back and transition into the back half of a loop.

6. After completing the loop, regain your entry airspeed, go back to step #2, and do it again. (When you do this maneuver the first time, you can recover at this point, making it half of a figure 8.)

Common errors and corrections

-   **Ending at an altitude that is significantly different than entry altitude**. If you end at a lower altitude, think about floating a little longer over the top of the half-loop to reduce your speed. Another factor could be that your upline was shallower than 45°. If you recover at a higher altitude (less common), you might be extending your 45° upline too long, or pulling too hard on the backside of your half-loop.

-   **Recovering from a heading off the point**. Letting a wing drop is the common culprit. Glance at both wingtips on your upline, check them again when rounding the top of the half-loop, and as you are recovering from the half-loop. Those are points where a quick wing adjustment is easiest.

3. 2-Turn Spin

Ending any lesson with a spin is always optional.

You probably noticed that I included an optional spin at the end of the last few lessons. That's for two reasons: 1) to productively use up altitude that you won't need to regain because you are heading back to the airport, and 2) to add an additional half-turn so you can get experience recovering from multiple rotations and higher rotation speeds. But if you feel physically or mentally strained, you should opt out of ending the lesson with a spin. Just enjoy your flight back to the airport and do your spinning some other day when you feel excited about it. You always want to leave a lesson looking forward to the next one, not thinking "Whew, I'm glad that's over." Your tolerance for extreme attitude flying will increase with practice, but even airshow pilots and aerobatic competitors avoid unproductively over-taxing themselves during practices, and so should you.

Practice with your homemade spin simulator

As I mentioned before in this book, a good way to review spin recoveries is to sit in a chair and simulate the process a few times, imagining that you have a stick and rudder pedals. Make this simulation all the more realistic by using a yard stick or baseball bat for the stick. Better yet, sit in the cockpit while it's in the hangar, and use the actual controls.

Do this exercise a minute or two each day for a week. Unlike most aerobatic maneuvers, spin recoveries are more about procedures and timing, rather than about form and ground reference points. Just to illustrate that point, I hypothetically might be able to teach a non-pilot how to recover from a spin, but I most certainly could not teach a non-pilot how to perform a slow roll.

How it's done, where to look

The entry and recovery of any spin is the same, but you'll need to start recovery sooner when the number of revolutions increase. For a 2-turn spin in a Super Decathlon, for example, I start recovery at the 1½-turn point, but it might be different in the make and model of airplane you are flying.

Remember to call out aloud your half-turn points:

"half"

"One"

"One-and-a half" [Start recovering at this point]

"Two" [You should be at your entry heading.]

As with any spin, you won't have time to say aloud the recovery procedure while doing it, or even think too much about it, so review your recovery sequence mentally before your flight lesson:

Power to idle (if it's not already)

Ailerons neutral

Full opposite **rudder**

Stick briskly forward just past neutral

Pull up with elevator from the dive and gradually add power to cruise

Common errors and corrections

- **Rolling out before or after your exit heading**. Lead time for the recovery depends on the particular airplane you are flying, and how quickly, correctly, and deliberately you apply the controls. To exit precisely from a multi-turn spin, you'll have to work fast. You can often peg your recovery point when you briskly push the stick past neutral to break the stall.

- **The spin/stall recovery seemed sluggish**. Remember that opposite rudder slows and stops the spin, and forward pressure on the stick reduces the angle of attack and stops the stall. Power above idle and aileron usage can aggravate the stall/spin and inhibit the recovery. Begin stopping the rotation at your recovery point with the rudder, and stop the stall with forward stick. With some practice, you'll be able to recover exactly at your exit point.

- **The rotation and airspeed increased rapidly during my recovery**. If your aircraft is rotating and the airspeed is quickly climbing, you are likely rolling and turning downward in a spiral. Instead of autorotating, you are diving in a steeply banked turn. Pulling back harder on the stick will only tighten the turns and exacerbate the rotation rate. Your wings are not stalled. They are flying, so you must roll out with ailerons and coordinated rudder, and then pull out of the resulting dive with the stick. Don't jerk or yank on the controls during a spiral, because opposing, twisting forces might damage the aircraft. If you exceeded the airplane's maximum airspeed or think you might have overstressed the airframe, you should have a licensed aircraft mechanic check the airplane before it is flown again.

- **The wings stalled during the recovery pullup**. You either pulled up too soon, too hard, or both before the airspeed increased.

- **I entered an outside spin during the recovery**. This is a rare error, but it's possible to cross over into an outside spin if you push the stick way too far forward without stopping rotation. Such an event is appropriately called a *crossover spin*. The way to recover is to stop rotation with opposite rudder and pull the stick back past neutral. In other words, follow the standard outside spin recovery procedure you learned in a previous lesson.

Lesson 9 – Airshow Favorites

Hammerhead Turn, 4-Point Slow Roll

The objectives of this lesson

1. Maintain spatial orientation while flying a vertical upline and reverse the direction by yawing into a vertical downline (hammerhead).

2. Use cross-control inputs to maintain the airplane's attitude during a 180° yaw turn.

3. Anticipate, prevent, and recover from an unintended tail slide or outside spin.

4. Pause at four points during a slow roll.

1. Hammerhead Turn

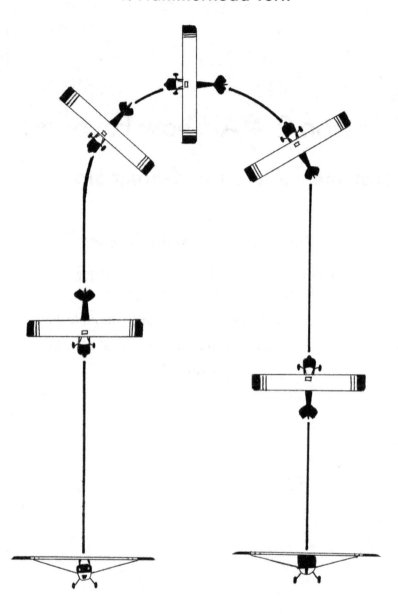

The hammerhead turn was a byproduct of early tail slide demonstrations. The first tail slide was performed in 1912 by Will Rhodes Moorhouse in a Radley & Moorhouse monoplane, powered by the popular 50 hp Gnome engine. His purpose was to demonstrate the strength and reliability of his airplane design during an extreme flight attitude. He entered the maneuver by pulling up into a vertical upline and then he cut the engine. When the airplane reached its highest point and started sliding backward toward the earth, it would yaw sideways, perhaps with the push of a rudder pedal, and drop into a dive. This must have been a crowd-gasping stunt back then, especially because Moorhouse's airplane looked like nothing more than a box kite with a motor on the front end. Later pilots would advance and enhance the sideways yaw with deliberate rudder pressure just before sliding backward, a maneuver then referred to as a "stall turn," and later a "hammerhead stall." Those titles were misnomers, however, because the wing wasn't stalled, even when in a tail slide—it was simply sliding backward. Today we call it a hammerhead turn, or just a hammerhead for short.

I took an aerobatic course in 1967, in a Beech Musketeer Sport, and during the second lesson the instructor demonstrated a hammerhead turn. It was certainly too early in the syllabus for me to perform that maneuver, but looking straight up and then straight down through the windshield of an airplane topped any rollercoaster ride I'd ever been on. Luckily, I happened to love rollercoasters, so I was thrilled and eager to learn more aerobatic maneuvers.

To perform a hammerhead, you would pull the airplane up as if entering a loop, stop pulling when the airplane is flying straight up (vertical upline), push full rudder to yaw over from the upline to a vertical downline, and pull out of the dive to a heading 180° from your entry heading. Ideally, the entry and exit altitude should be close, but just concentrate on proper and timely control inputs for now.

As with all aerobatic maneuvers, check your POH for the recommended hammerhead entry speed for your aircraft. You'll need enough momentum to maintain a vertical upline long enough to start the yaw turn. I've flown hammerheads in an aerobatic glider, and I had to extend my dive for a sufficient entry speed. The long wings and a long fuselage were hard to swing around, I had to hold the rudder down for quite a while to make the engineless nose eventually yaw over into a dive. I had just ridden a nice thermal up to about 8,000 feet AGL, so I had plenty of airspace with which to do a series of these graceful hammerheads on the way back to the airport.

How it's done, where to look

1. Like with a loop, performing this maneuver over a straight road will help you maintain your spatial orientation. It can be a short road because you'll be going straight up, and then straight down. After establishing the entry speed recommended in your airplane's POH, notice your entry point, and pull up as if you were entering humpty bump.

2. Glance at your wingtips. When they are 90° to, and equidistant from, the horizon

you'll be in a straight-up vertical line. You need to work fast because your airspeed will quickly deteriorate.

3. Push full rudder in the desired direction of your yaw. As the nose arcs down sideways, the outside wing (the one pointing up) is flying through more air molecules than the downward wing, which makes the faster-moving upward wing want to roll you over inverted. To correct this rollover tendency, roll the wing back with your ailerons, which means pulling the stick in the opposite direction of your rudder input. You will be cross-controlled until you establish your downline.

4. When your speed starts to increase, the nose will want to come up. Keep your downline straight with forward stick pressure. At this point in a left yaw, for example, your stick will be to the right and forward—most likely, in fact, all the way to the right and all the way forward. This, combined with full opposite rudder, makes you susceptible to an inadvertent outside spin. When your nose is coming down, however, you'll gain airspeed and reduce your vulnerability.

5. As soon as you've established a downline, recover by gradually pulling up to straight and level flight—not too abruptly at low speed or you might stall. Your exit heading should be 180° from your entry heading.

Common errors and corrections

- **Exiting at an altitude substantially different from the entry altitude**. It could be because your recovery pullup was too quick or too slow. The most common reason, though, is unequal upline and downline. I learned a trick from a friend who was an aerobatic instructor, and also an orchestra percussionist. He kept his uplines and downlines equal by counting beats throughout the maneuver, like this: pull to vertical upline ("one, two"), yaw to vertical downline ("one, two"), pull to straight and level.

- **Recovering at a heading other than 180° from the entry heading**. A likely reason is that the "top" wing created lift during your yaw turn, and you didn't compensate with opposite aileron. That wing is moving through more air than the lower wing, so the airplane wants to roll the up wing more than it does into the low wing. If you don't correct the rolling differential, it will affect your exit heading. You counter that tendency by moving the stick toward the opposite side of the rudder you are pushing, just enough to keep the wing from rolling inverted. In other words, you'll be cross-controlled (uncoordinated) during the yaw turn. Keep the nose coming down to gain some airspeed, so you don't stall or spin.

- **The airplane went into an outside spin during the yaw turn**. During the yaw turn, your airspeed is very low, and you are pushing on the stick and moving it to the side opposite of the pressed rudder—full rudder one way, ailerons the other way, and pushing on the stick—that's the formula for an outside spin. And now you know why learning how to recover from an outside spin was covered in this curriculum before introducing you to the hammerhead.

- **The airplane buffeted when pulling up from the downline**. Unintended inside stalls happen more frequently during hammerheads than unintended outside spins, but when either of them occurs with me in the airplane, my student gets to experience an airplane stalling even while diving straight down toward the ground. The common reason for an inside stall during the downline, of course, is pulling back on the stick too vigorously and/or too soon, and exceeding critical AOA. Airspeed will build quickly on the downline, so you can soon pull out of the dive without stalling.

- **The airplane hesitated to yaw-turn**. Your airspeed was either too low over the top, and/or you didn't apply full rudder for the yaw turn. Airspeed deteriorates rapidly on the upline, so as soon as you've confirmed that you are going straight up with a glance at your wingtips, immediately start your yaw turn with full rudder. If you hesitate too long on the upline, your airspeed might be too slow for a nice U-shape. The airplane will just mush over onto its side and then eventually point toward the ground. From the ground, instead of that looking like a U-shape, it would look the airplane is heading back down through the same vertical line. Spectators won't notice or care, but competition judges will.

- **The airplane would not yaw-turn, but the nose eventually flipped downward**. To complete that scenario, the nose likely would have then wobbled pendulum-like until increased airspeed gave you control authority to pull out of the dive. If you didn't have enough airspeed for the rudder to yaw the airplane, or if you were in a tail slide and didn't realize it, the nose will eventually point downward, but probably not the way you are expecting.

A Word or Two About Unintended Tail Slides

A tail slide is a condition where the airplane slides backward down a vertical line. You should not do them on purpose unless your airplane is approved for them, and even then, not until you've been checked out by a competent aerobatic CFI.

Even if your airspeed becomes zero on the upline of a maneuver, the nose will eventually fall one way or the other. A sustained tail slide requires an exact backward downline, which is very challenging to control. It's like throwing a dart straight up, and expecting it to slide backward for a few seconds before the heavy tip drops down and points toward the ground.

Fat chance. It's also very challenging to know just when you are actually tail sliding. When I'm performing tail slides or torque rolls in an airplane approved for them, I rely on a footlong strand of yarn tied to a strut. With the even slightest whiff of airspeed, the yarn continues pointing backward, but the moment a tailslide starts, the yarn immediately points forward. Tailslide entries are virtually undetectable without that little piece of yarn.

I already mentioned that intended tail slides are very hard to sustain. The next time you are at an airshow, watch how long the pilot slides backward during a torque roll (i.e., rolling during the upline and continuing to roll in the same direction by changing the direction of the ailerons while sliding backward). The nose usually drops out of the maneuver pretty quickly.

If you think you might be close to, or actual in, a tail sliding, push full rudder either way, and the airplane will gradually fall to one side. If you really are in a tail slide, the airplane will fall to the side opposite of your rudder pressure. That's because the wind is hitting your rudder's surface from behind, producing an opposite effect. Similarly, I don't advocate pulling on the stick if you think you might be tail sliding. First, most large aerobatic airplane rudders will catch more wind than the elevator, hence, giving you more control authority. Second, if you are tail sliding and you pull back on the stick, the airplane will aggressively pitch forward, and that would give you a negative-G experience that could be alarming (or a lot of fun, depending on your disposition).

2. 4-Point Roll

A 4-point roll is a slow roll that you pause at knife edge, then again when inverted, stop at knife edge and again on the other side, and then roll back to normal flight. By "pause," I mean to completely stop rolling at each point, wait one second, two at the most, and then continue rolling to the next point.

Practicing 4-point rolls is a great way to improve your spatial orientation and also a good way to improve your control inputs during a slow roll. You're not ready to be a show pilot at this point in the curriculum, but a 4-point roll does look cool from the ground, even when you're at a high altitude. My aerobatic practice area is over rural Minnesota, and I've often wondered if farmers sometimes look up from their tractors for a free high-altitude airshow.

You already know how to slow roll and how to stop inverted. For the knife edge stops, remember to use "up" rudder to prevent the heavy nose from dropping too soon. You might want to review the slow roll steps in the previous lesson, and pay attention to the common errors and suggested remedies for them. As always when rolling, watch your point on the horizon and focus on making your nose remain equidistant from it.

How it's done, where to look

1. Choose a reference point on the horizon, and enter a slow roll. When you get to a 90° bank (knife edge), neutralize the ailerons while adding full opposite rudder to hold the nose up. Keep pushing on the stick or the airplane will want to turn into your reference point.

2. After a very quick pause (i.e., one or two seconds), roll inverted and neutralize your ailerons and rudders when your wings are level in relation to the horizon. As with any inverted flight, you'll need plenty of pushing on the stick to hold the nose above your reference point.

3. After a quick pause, roll to the other knife edge side, and neutralize your ailerons. Use full rudder to hold the nose up. Continue pushing on the stick or the airplane will want to turn into the point.

4. After a quick pause, roll with coordinated rudder to normal flight.

Common errors and corrections

- **The nose drops toward the ground during knife edge**. Unless your airplane has a tremendous power-to-weight ratio, full rudder will not keep the nose up for very long. There just isn't enough lift produced from the side of the fuselage. The remedy is to make your knife edge stops *very* brief. It's probably better for the engine, too, because oil distribution is less efficient when it's on its side.

- **The nose didn't make a perfect circle around the reference point**. The best remedy is to practice 4-point rolls until you can make a perfect circle around your reference point. At this point in your learning, however, if you kept the point in sight throughout the maneuver, call it a success. This is a complex maneuver, requiring many of the skills you've learned so far. Be patient and have fun practicing.

Lesson 10 – Quick Action Maneuvers

Snap Roll, Hammerhead with Vertical Half-Rolls

The objectives of this lesson

1. Perform an accelerated horizontal spin (snap roll) while remaining spatially oriented during a fast-moving and erratic attitude change.
2. Experience how an airplane can stall and spin from straight-and-level flight with aggressive control inputs.
3. Apply simultaneous and rapid roll inputs during a hammerhead upline and again during the downline.

1. Snap Roll

Snap rolls are technically horizontal accelerated spins. They were called autorotational rolls circa 1913, and eventually named flick rolls in Great Britain. During World War I aerial dogfights, RAF pilots used flick rolls to shake off enemy pilots who were gunning them from behind. The flick roll's wild gyrations, which eventually dropped into a downward vertical spin, made it almost impossible for German pilots to get a gunsight bead on an RAF pilot tumbling chaotically through the sky. Today we call them snap rolls in the US, and they are exciting to perform, even without an enemy on your tail.

You've learned a few different ways to roll an airplane, but because the snap roll is actually an accelerated ("snapped into") spin, it's yawing roll is induced by full rudder and a full pullback on the stick. Like with any other spin, it's a stall because you'll have the stick full back to exceed the critical angle of attack. It rolls because full rudder makes one wing stall deeper than the other—chasing the other wing around, so to speak. (By the way, you've no doubt noticed, to the chagrin of tech-oriented pilots—and there are a lot of them—that

I seldom use scientific jargon when explaining how one thing effects other things during aerobatic flight. It's a habit I've picked up over the years. I've had to explain complex maneuvers accurately, and sometimes expediently, in a way that's quick and easy to grasp.)

Because the snap roll, as with other spins, is a timing maneuver more than a coordinated stick-and-rudder maneuver, it might seem simple: simply push a rudder all the way in and pull the stick all the way back, then apply opposite control inputs to recover. That's how you get into and out of a spin, right? But performing a correct snap roll is extra challenging because it happens fast, the yawing is erratic, and recovery requires quick control inputs. That's why this maneuver appears toward the end of the curriculum, after you've developed aerobatic skills in a variety of maneuvers, especially spins.

As with all aerobatic maneuvers, use the entry speed recommended by your airplane's manufacturer. You don't want excessive airspeed because high speed twisting could put a huge strain on the airplane.

You might hear other pilots say you have to *yank* the stick and *kick* the rudder for a snap roll. But as I've said before, you shouldn't yank or kick anything on an airplane, especially control surfaces that can stall or twist with that kind of abuse. You want to feel your foot pushing against the rudder (you won't if you kick it), and you want to feel your hand(s) pulling the stick straight back (you won't if you yank it). On the other hand, you do want to *expediently* pull full back on the stick and *expediently* push on the rudder pedal. You want a crisp entry, not sluggish one.

How it's done, where to look

1. **Set your entry speed and attitude.** Set your throttle wherever recommended by your aircraft's POH, which is often cruise power, and use the manufacturer's recommended entry speed. You can climb to reduce speed or dive slightly to increase speed, but then enter the snap roll from a level attitude. Make sure your ailerons remain neutral throughout the maneuver—this is a spin, not a roll. (As you already know, I like to pull the stick back with both hands to make sure I'm not inadvertently tugging it to one side.)

2. **Initiate the snap roll.** When you reach your entry speed and attitude, pull straight back rapidly on the stick, and while the stick is coming full back, step fully on a rudder. The outside wing will rise (lift) and the inside wing will drop (stall), and the resulting yaw-roll will continue as long as you push on that rudder and hold back on the stick.

3. **Recover from the snap roll.** On most aerobatic airplanes, you'll need to start recovering as soon as the airplane rolls inverted. Recover with full opposite rudder,

immediately followed by forward stick past neutral, enough to stop the stall and recover with the wings level. The nose will likely end up below the horizon, but that's okay. This is a timing maneuver, so ending the snap roll with the wings level is more important. (See the tip in the first "common error" description below.)

Common errors and corrections

- **The airplane yawed erratically during the snap roll.** I have good news for you: that's normal. This isn't a true roll, it's a spin, which is a yaw-roll combination. If you want to tame the yawing a bit when the snap roll starts, let off on the stick back pressure a *little* to decrease the angle of attack. You should remain stalled, but not as deeply. (This tip will be helpful in the next lesson when you perform a maneuver called the *avalanche*, which is a snap roll on the top of a loop.)

- **The airplane mushed into the snap roll.** Hesitant stick and rudder inputs will result in a sloppy snap roll, and maybe one that simply falls into a regular stall or downward spin. Brisk entry control inputs make the snap roll snappier. If you do fall into a regular spin, however, immediately bring your throttle back to idle to prevent a flat spin (more about flat spins in a moment), and recover as you usually would from the spin.

- **I recovered past wings-level.** Start your recovery sooner next time, and/or make your recovering rudder and stick inputs brisker. Also, try a bit more forward pressure on the stick when you recover, just enough to make sure the angle of attack on both wings is sufficiently reduced, but not enough to induce negative angle of attack and crossover into an outside spin. (There is such a thing as an outside snap roll, but not in this curriculum.)

- **The airplane rolled so fast that everything was a blur.** That's normal at first, but for some reason our sensory perceptions eventually speed up with repeated exposure to a maneuver. This phenomenon will gradually make the maneuver seem slower.

A Word or Two About Unintended Flat Spins

I once inadvertently put a Cessna Aerobat into a flat spin while doing snap rolls. The flight school I instructed at was a Cessna dealer, and I encouraged the owner to buy an Aerobat the first year they were introduced to the market. Since I was the only CFI at the school with aerobatic experience, plus hundreds of Cessna 150 hours as an instructor, the owner gave me enough free solo flight time to familiarize myself with the airplane's characteristics. I found the snap rolls to be crisp and quick, and sometimes I held the airplane into a series of revolutions until the nose finally dropped into a normal spin. But one day, even though the rolling stopped, the nose didn't drop down. It continued yawing perpetually around the horizon with the wings level. None of my controls had any effect. I finally remembered that the power was still at the cruise setting. As soon as I pulled it back to idle, the nose dropped into a normal spin, and I was able to quickly recover.

When I started giving aerobatic instruction in the Aerobat, I made sure my students always remembered the "P" (power to idle) in the "PARE" spin recovery acronym. I did this by having them touch the throttle, although it was already at idle, when recovering from a spin, just to keep the automatic sequence intact.

Several years later, I mentioned my flat spin incident to the great aerobatic champion and instructor, Bill Thomas, when he was giving me some advanced spin and aerobatic instructor training in his Pitts S-2B. He said the same thing happened to him in an Aerobat. We both admitted to it being a startling surprise, but reducing power had been the cure for both of us. I've never heard of unintended flat spins happen like this in any other aircraft, or by any other pilots.

In a flat spin, the airstream against the bottom of your airplane prevents sufficient control surface airflow to make them effective. When you bring the power back to idle, the heavy nose will no longer be held up by the propeller's gyroscopic precession ("torque"), and the nose should drop down into a normal spin, provided your ailerons are neutral.

While we're on the topic of flat spins, if the center of gravity has been moved backward too far due to excessive aft weight, some weight might have to be shifted forward to recover from a flat spin. As I've said before, I can't imagine a more challenging situation. To make sure that never happens, always calculate your weight and balance before every flight, making sure they are within the approved envelope. That calculation should be as important as checking for sufficient fuel and oil for the flight.

2. Hammerhead with 2 Half-Rolls

You already know how to fly a hammerhead, and this maneuver will introduce you to jazzing it up by rolling on the vertical lines, both up and down. You should first learn this maneuver with half-rolls for two reasons: 1) keeping straight uplines and downlines while rolling is challenging at first; 2) most aerobatic training airplanes only have enough power and momentum to maintain a vertical upline for a very short time.

How it's done, where to look

1. **Entry airspeed.** For this maneuver, I like to enter with a bit more airspeed than for a normal hammerhead turn. I want all the energy oomph I can get to make a straight-up half roll. Even with that extra momentum energy, you'll have to work fast.

2. **Roll 180° on the upline.** After pulling up, glance at your wings and as soon as you've achieved a vertical upline, and with wings equidistant from the horizon, apply full aileron in one direction, and neutralize the ailerons as soon as you've rolled 180°. You won't need rudder because there won't be any adverse yaw. Glance at the horizon during your roll for reference (looking straight up at blue sky doesn't give you much orientation information).

3. **Yaw into the hammerhead turn.** Immediately apply full rudder to yaw toward the direction you want to turn.

4. **Roll 180° on the downline.** Glance at your wings again and when you reach the vertical downline, immediately apply your ailerons in either direction, and neutralize when you've rolled 180°.

5. **Pull to recover.** After completing the final half roll, start pulling out of the dive. You should be heading in the direction opposite of your entry heading. (If you only rolled on the upline or the downline, you will end up heading in the same direction as your entry. Work that out sometime on the ground with your hand or a toy airplane.)

Common errors and corrections

- **I got confused and then botched the maneuver.** If your spatial orientation gets fouled up, abort the maneuver by pointing the nose down and flying out of it. A good way to get the nose down if you are on an upline is with full rudder to one side. If you end up in an inverted dive, you should know by now what to do: Push to stabilize the dive and roll out. "*Push-and-Roll.*" Then gradually pull out of your right-side-up dive. Don't try to split-S out of an inverted dive, or you might exceed your airspeed limitation, lose way too much altitude, and/or pull too many Gs during the pullout.

- **I got disoriented during my upline half-roll.** It's easy to lose track of where you are in the upline roll, especially when looking straight up at a blue sky. Instead, look at how your wingtips are moving around the horizon.

- **I didn't exit the maneuver at my entry heading.** You likely stopped one of your rolls too soon or too late.

Lesson 11 – Advanced Spin Recovery

Avalanche, 2½ Turn Spin

The objectives of this lesson

Blend a coordinated maneuver (loop) with an accelerated spin maneuver (snap roll).

1. Identify physiological reactions from multi-turn spins.

2. Maintain spatial orientation, and make precision recoveries from multi-turning, fast-rotating spins.

1. Avalanche

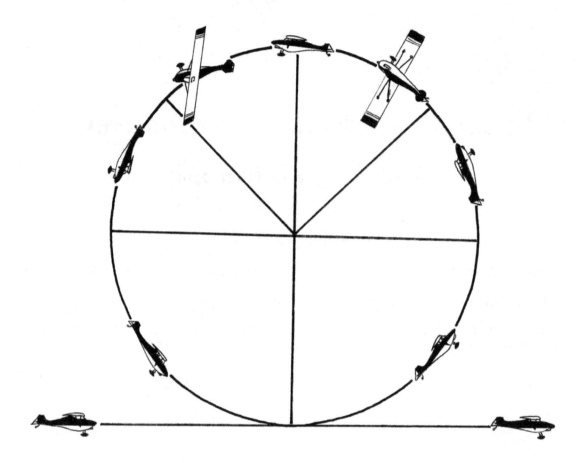

The avalanche is performed by completing a snap roll on top of a loop. You'll enter a tight loop to make sure you have enough airspeed on the top to make a complete snap roll, and then exit like with any other loop.

How it's done, where to look

1. Check your airplane POH to see if it has a recommended entry speed for an avalanche. It's doubtful you'll find anything, though, because this is a combined maneuver—a loop and a snap roll. I start the loop in a Super Decathlon with the same entry speed and G-force that I would for an Immelmann.

2. As with any loop, relax a little back pressure on the stick to round out the top of the loop after the nose tips back into inverted flight.

3. As soon as the nose passes through the inverted position, check your airspeed and

when it's at your snap roll entry speed, push one of the rudders full in and pull the stick all the way straight back. As soon as the airplane breaks into a snap roll, ease the stick forward just a little, but keep the rudder full in.

4. Start your snap roll recovery just as you begin to roll right-side up on top of the loop. You want to be recovered by the time you return to inverted flight to complete the loop. Let the nose come down and when you have enough airspeed, complete the last quarter of the loop.

Common errors and corrections

- **The wings just buffeted and the nose fell out of the loop**. If that happens, abort the maneuver by pointing the nose down to pick up airspeed and pull out of the dive. If the dive is inverted push and roll before pulling out to avoid a split-S. The culprit for that failed snap roll could have been using less than full rudder and insufficient backpressure to enter the snap roll, but it's more likely that you didn't have enough entry airspeed for anything but a sluggish stall that drained your lift. Next time, make sure your loop entry speed is sufficient by pulling hard during the first quarter of the loop, and start your snap roll as soon as your nose starts going inverted at the top of the loop, and you've reached your snap roll entry speed.

- **The snap roll fell into a spin.** If your airplane's nose starts to point down into a regular spin during the snap roll, you already know the recovery drill: pull the throttle to idle, ailerons neutral, full opposite rudder, stick forward just past neutral.

- **The snap roll didn't recover inverted**. If you rolled out past inverted, start your recovery sooner next time, almost as soon as the snap roll begins. If you rolled out before inverted, delay your recovery a little. That advice is easy to give, but I know it's hard to time the recovery because things are happening fast.

- **The exit altitude from the loop was substantially lower than the entry altitude**. As soon as you recover from the snap roll, let the nose come down and add back pressure as soon as you have sufficient airspeed (you don't want a secondary stall at this point). Remember, you are still looping, so you'll need to pull about the same G-forces on the last quarter of the loop as you did on the first quarter.

2. The 2 ½ Turn Spin

As I've mentioned before, each airplane has its own spin signature. A typical example would be accelerating the rotation rate for the first four turns, and then stabilizing for a while into a slower rate of rotation because centrifugal force lifts the nose a little, but then the nose yaws over after a few turns into a steeper downline, and the cycle starts all over again. That spin signature could closely define either the Cessna Aerobat or the Super Decathlon. Ask your instructor about the multiple-turn spin characteristics of the airplane you are learning aerobatics in.

The 2½ turn spin will be an opportunity to notice if you experience any of the physiological reactions that are covered at the end of this lesson plan.

How it's done, where to look

1. Enter a spin at a higher altitude than for one-turn spins (i.e., an extra 1000 feet). Notice your entry heading and altitude.
2. As always, count each half-turn point aloud; i.e., *half…one…one-and-a-half… two…two-and-a-half.* You'll be counting fast, but it will help you stay oriented.
3. Initiate your recovery at the "*two*" point and completely recover at the "*two-and-a-half*" point.
4. After recovering, pull out of the dive and notice your heading and altitude loss.

Common errors and corrections

*   **Not exiting at a heading that's 180° from the entry heading.** Next time, either advance or delay your recovery initiation point, depending on whether you rolled out before or after you entrance point. Make sure you are using full opposite rudder, and briskly move the stick forward just past neutral to nail the heading. The most common error, however, is simply losing track of the number of turns, which is likely if you are not counting aloud by half-turns. Remember, when you say "two," start recovering.

*   **Losing count of the turns.** Whenever you lose track of your turns, recover immediately. *If you lose your orientation, you are losing control of your airplane.* Don't worry, though, because your situational awareness will get better with some practice. You might remember that even a one-turn spin was somewhat of a blur the first time. The way to keep track of turns is to always count by half-turns aloud, even when you are practicing solo.

Common Physiological Effects from Spins

Sensory signals can affect your mental perception of what the airplane is doing, both during the spin and after you've recovered. Let's look at a few of those physiological factors.

Vertigo

In the avalanche maneuver, you might have felt a little dizzy afterward. That's because you—or, specifically, your head—accelerated, decelerated, and moved through multiple 3-dimentional planes in quick succession. Similarly, if you perform a lot of turning maneuvers, one after the other, you might get dizzy and confused, a condition called *vertigo*. If you want a sample of this on the ground, sit securely in a swivel chair with arm rests to steady yourself. (Have someone with you who can keep you from falling out of the chair.) With your eyes open, spin around three or four times. During the last turn, nod your head up and down once or twice and then stop quickly while holding the armrests. Notice how you feel. You might feel unstable, and it might feel like you are still spinning. That's vertigo. Wait until your perceptions settle down before getting up from the chair.

Vertigo is a natural reaction to mixed signals that come from the semicircular canals inside your inner ear, which are designed to help you detect movement. One of the semicircular canals reacts when you rotate your head from one side to the other or when you are completely turning, another reacts when you move your head toward one shoulder then the other, and one reacts when you nod up and down. In other words, they detect yaw, roll, and pitch movements. While you are moving your head one way or the other, an oily fluid inside each semicircular canal moves past tiny sensitive hairs. These hairs send an electrical message to the brain to warn you that you are moving in a certain direction. But when you stop moving, the fluid's momentum can continue giving you the false perception that you are still moving. For example, when you stop a spin, the fluid inside the sensing semicircular canal continues flowing for a moment, sending a false message to your brain that you are still spinning, even though you're not. This misperception has led pilots to keep pressing the opposite rudder too long during their spin recovery, resulting in a secondary spin to the other direction. The way to override this misperception is to fix your eyes on something on the ground to "prove" to your brain that you are no longer spinning. If you watch a video of a ballet dancer whirling around on her toe in a pirouette, you'll see her quickly moving her head to keep track of a single point of reference. (Nothing more unstable than a dizzy dancer.)

Nystagmus

If you are walking and then trip, falling, say, to your left side, your eyes will automatically flick to the left to help you find something to either grab or to safely land on. In a 1965 study reported by the FAA's Office of Aviation Medicine, Civil Aeromedical Research Institute, the eye movements of ice figure skaters were sometimes found to keep moving after recovering from multi-turn rotations. Their eyes continued darting involuntarily toward the direction of the spin even though the skater had just stopped spinning. The affected skaters reported this as blurred vision and the illusion they were still spinning, a condition technically known as *nystagmus*. The skaters were able to override this blurring by fixing their gaze on something stationary for a moment after they stopped spinning.

Nystagmus can also make a pilot who has just recovered from a spin, and especially from a multi-turn spin, think that she is continuing to spin even though rotation has actually stopped. This could lead to over-holding the opposite rudder, and then inadvertently spinning in the opposite direction. The prevention, as with the ice skaters, is to look at a fixed reference point on the ground.

As an aside, another interesting finding from that FAA study was that when the skaters were allowed to choose either direction to spin, seven of the eight skaters chose to spin to the left. Perhaps the overwhelming bias to turn left is the original reason why airport patterns generally require turns to the left. When I give aerobatic students a choice to make their first roll or spin either left or right, they usually choose left. Soldiers always start marching by stepping out on their left foot, and wilderness rescuers know that lost hikers tend to wander aimlessly toward the left. And so on, but I'll get back to the subject at hand.

Awe

An experience becomes *awesome* when you are overwhelmingly fascinated by it. Being fascinated can be a delight, but being overly awestruck during a multi-turn spin can severely distract your spatial orientation and situational awareness, making you lose track of your number of turns and your altitude—and just about everything else except the whirling ground you are staring at. That's why you should callout aloud each half-turn, even when flying solo. It's easy to lose track when just counting full turns, but counting half-turns requires keen focus and mental discipline (you want the maximum of both).

Confusion

When a student stops counting, or miscounts half-turns, I always say "Okay, recover." The airplane is taking control. After recovering, I asked those students how many turns they made, and they invariably guess fewer turns than they actually made. They also lost track of their altitude. That confusion impaired their ability to control the airplane. If you lose count of your half-turns, recover immediately.

If your plan is to spin down to a specific altitude, recover immediately upon reaching it. If you glance at your altimeter and feel even momentarily confused, recover immediately.

If you lose spatial orientation or situational awareness during any aerobatic maneuver, you've lost some control. Retake control by aborting the maneuver and redoing it from the beginning. When practicing, that's what champion aerobatic pilots do, it's what renowned airshow pilots do, and so should you.

Lesson 12 – Putting it All Together

Combinations and Sequences

The objectives of this lesson

1. Maintain and enhance spatial orientation under challenging cognitive demands.
2. Fly multiple maneuvers in a continuous sequence.
3. Improve rapid recall of maneuvers that have already been learned.

Choreographing a sequence

This is more than a simple review of maneuvers you've already learned—it is a chance to perform a series of those maneuvers in a choreographed sequence. This will place higher demands on your preparation, spatial awareness, and reaction time. It will also sharpen your new skills, help you retain them, and help you stay ahead of the airplane.

Instead of going through the mental gymnastics of first sorting out these sequences while flying them, simulate them on the ground with your hand as a model airplane before the flight—knuckles are the top, palm is the bottom—or better yet, use a toy airplane to visualize what the sequence will look like.

Take plenty of time to make thorough clearing turns before and between these sequences, and give yourself plenty of airspace for safety. Remember to start each maneuver in the sequence with the POH's recommended entry speed.

When you are flying from one maneuver to the next, make sure the altitude is safely high enough for the next maneuver, and that you have reached the next maneuver's entry speed before entering it. Mindfully concentrate on each maneuver at a time, and then concentrate fully on the next one, and so on. To help keep track, competition pilots clip or tape a schematic reference somewhere on the panel showing a standardized symbol for each maneuver in the sequence. You'll soon learn to read those standard maneuver symbols, known as *Aresti* symbols.

A Word or Two About Competition

The combinations in this lesson are not meant to be official competition sequences, which can change every year. I put these sequences together as educational exercises, generalized enough to help you later learn any set of sequences. If you plan to fly in an aerobatic contest, you should talk to your aerobatic flight instructor about some differences between recreational and competition aerobatic maneuvers. For example, the Immelmann in this course is taught as a half loop, a pause inverted, and then a half-roll to right-side up. It's a good way to learn the maneuver. In competition, however, that would be considered two maneuvers: half-loop, half-roll. The competition version of the Immelmann would require a more gradual rollout while still looping, timed so you would end rolling upright at the apogee of the loop, reaching your reference point with wings level. Another example is spin recovery. In competition, the judges like to see you establish a brief straight downline before pulling out of the recovery dive. In this course, you learned to always recover from a spin with minimum altitude loss. I wanted that reaction to be your automatic default, but you can easily alter that for the judges. I'll tell you more about competition a little later.

1. Four-Leaf Cloverleaf

The four-leaf cloverleaf is a good example of combining maneuvers together into one sequence. It will give you practice in setting up entry speeds from one maneuver to the next, keeping your loop exits at the same altitude, and managing your half-rolls to come out right. The sequence will start with the same cloverleaf you learned early in this curriculum, but with a few added twists.

How it's done, where to look

1. Choose an entry reference point on the horizon. If you're flying in an area with straight roads, entering the same direction as one of them will give you an added reference during your quarter-turn rollout on the backside. Otherwise, simply estimate a quarter-turn while glancing at the ground during the third quarter of the loop.
2. Enter a loop. The first half of the loop will be the same as the other loops you have practiced.

3. When your aircraft's nose starts coming down on the third quarter of the loop, start your quarter-roll. Continue adding back pressure on the stick, though, because you are still looping while turning.

4. As soon as you start rolling, look up to find a point 90° from your entry heading. Roll out on that point.

5. Instead of completely recovering to straight and level from the loop, dive to the loop entry speed, and start another loop. Complete steps 1-4 above to form another cloverleaf.

6. After your third cloverleaf, you might choose to recover to straight and level flight. If you made half-rolls to the left, your exit heading should be 90° to the left of your entry heading. If you felt adventurous enough for four cloverleaf loops, however, you should have exited at your initial entry heading.

Common errors and corrections

- **Not ending the sequence at the initial entry altitude**. That's a tough standard to meet at first. When practicing these in the future, you can shorten or extend your exit altitude at the end of each leaf by glancing at your airspeed. If you need more airspeed for the next loop's entry, ease off on backpressure, and if you want less airspeed, pull harder. This means your loops might not be perfectly round, but this is a training exercise, not a competition maneuver.

- **Not ending the sequence at the entry heading**. That's another tough standard that will likely give you plenty of room for improvement. It will help to use a ground reference to check your heading as the nose starts down from the apogee of each loop, and during each quarter-roll on the backside, aim for a 90° point.

2. Hammerhead Turn, Ending with a Slow Roll One Way and a Snap Roll the Other Way.

This sequence has two slow maneuvers (hammerhead and slow roll), ending with a very fast one (snap roll). You will first complete a hammerhead, and then do a slow roll one way, and then a snap roll in the other direction. Plan ahead for the heading and entry speed of each roll maneuver.

How it's done, where to look

1. Perform a hammerhead turn. During the recovery pullup, head for a point that's 180° from your hammerhead's entry heading.

2. Perform a slow roll when you've established your heading and entry speed. You can climb or dive to reach your entry speed, but then return to a straight and level for a second or two to signify your commencement of the roll.

3. After recovering from the roll, dive or climb to reach your spin entry speed, and return to straight and level for a second or two to commence a snap roll in the opposite direction of your slow roll.

Common errors and corrections

- **Losing track of entry headings.** You'll benefit from a reference on the ground, such as a road, railroad track, or farm field section line. Choosing magnetic corrections won't do you much good in an aerobatic airplane because they generally don't have gyro direction indicators, and the magnetic compass will be sloshing around too much. While finishing one maneuver, try to make minor heading corrections for the next maneuver.

- **Botching one maneuver, which cascades into a poor performance on the next maneuver(s).** If you mess up a maneuver, fix it as best you can, but then forget it and concentrate on your next maneuver. If you are in competition and you flub one maneuver but get the other two right, you'll still earn points. If, on the other hand, your error puts you into an inverted dive, a spin, or some other upset, abort the entire sequence and start from scratch.

3. Two-Turn Spin, and an Immelmann rolled out in the Opposite Direction

This sequence is balanced in a few different ways. A low-G maneuver is followed by a high-G maneuver, lost altitude from the spin is regained in the Immelmann, a fast maneuver is balanced by a slow maneuver, rotating in one direction is followed by rolling in the opposite direction, and you'll end up 180° from your original entry heading. That's balancing a lot of extreme angles and changing speeds, and it gives you a lot to do in a short period of time. You'll also get an excellent spatial orientation workout.

All that turning and rolling carries the potential of the physiological effects I discussed previously, such as vertigo and nystagmus. You can override those effects by focusing on your ground reference points. Doing that will give your brain the information it needs to understand what you actually see, instead of what your physiology is falsely reporting.

How it's done, where to look

1. **Make a normal spin entry.** (I don't still have to remind you to count by half-turns, do I?) At the "one-and-a-half" point start recovering with opposite rudder, and stop at the "two" point with forward stick.

2. **Make any needed heading adjustments** during your recovery pullup, and time the pullup so you end at or close to the Immelmann entry speed.

3. **Enter a normal Immelmann,** and recover by rolling out of inverted flight in a direction opposite of your spin. In other words, if you entered your spin to the left, roll upright from the Immelmann to the right.

4. **Notice your heading** (it should be 180° from your spin entry heading) and note how close your exit altitude is to your spin entry altitude.

Common errors and corrections

1. **Not ending the Immelmann 180° from the spin entry heading.** Next time monitor your beginning and ending points more carefully and make adjustments as needed after the spin recovery and pullup, and during the Immelmann recovery. Check your wingtips during your Immelmann loop. That's easier said than done, though, with all that rolling and direction changing.

2. **Getting mixed up during the sequence.** All those balancing factors I talked about before explaining this sequence meant lots of attitude, heading, and speed changes. If those factors become hopelessly unbalanced, abort the maneuver and have a good chuckle. I'm reminded about the pilot who planned to do a series of three snap rolls on top of a loop, but he reached the apogee of the loop with too much airspeed for either a snap roll or to pull through the second half of the loop (i.e., the equivalent of a split-S with too much airspeed). He appropriately aborted the maneuver by pushing into an inverted dive after passing through the loop's apogee, and then rolled upright. Easy breezy. You know the story: he did the same thing again and named it the Cuban 8.

New sky-bound adventures

There's no end to the combinations you can put together, as long as you stick to the maneuvers recommended by the aircraft manufacturer. I sometimes mentally invent new iterations while driving or going for a walk.

Lesson 13 – Introducing Competition

The sport of aerobatic flying is generally classified into three camps: recreational, competition, and airshow. That breakdown might suggest that there are three types of aerobatic pilots, but it's been my experience that pilots who compete or fly airshow gigs also fly aerobatics just for the fun of it.

Regardless of your aerobatic interests, I suggest you consider membership in the International Aerobatic Club (IAC), which sanctions aerobatic contests in various locations. The IAC also publishes an outstanding aerobatic magazine called Sport Aerobatics that appeals to all levels and types of aerobatic interests and abilities. If you attend one of their competitions, you'll compete in a category or your choice. Those categories are Primary, Sportsman, Intermediate, Advanced, and Unlimited, each level increasingly more challenging, and perhaps, at some point, requiring an airplane with more power and responsiveness than the aerobatic trainer you've been flying. If you have completed flight training for the lessons in this curriculum, you should be competent to compete in either the Primary or Sportsman level. I recommend that you first attend a competition just to watch and get acquainted with the event and meet other pilots (bring a portable chair). I also recommend that you fly with someone who has competed at an aerobatic contest, mostly to get used to flying a designated series of maneuvers above a small geographic area known as the "box."

The aerobatic box is a block of airspace 1,000 meters (3,281 feet) long by 1,000 meters wide, and is identified by landmarks that you must fly within. The maximum and minimum AGL heights of this box depend on which aerobatic category you are competing in. If you go outside the box's boundaries, the contest judges will deduct points from your performance.

The required sequence of maneuvers you'll need to train for are periodically changed, and are represented graphically in shorthand schematics known as Aresti symbols, so named from the Aresti Catalog of the *Fédération Aéronautique Internationale* (FAI). The symbols were created by Spanish pilot Colonel José Luis Aresti Aguirre (1919–2003). Each symbol includes schematics of lines, arrows, and numbers. With those symbols, an entire sequence of maneuvers can be depicted on a card or sheet of paper and affixed to available space on your instrument panel for quick reference.

I'll give you a short tour of how to read Aresti symbols, and then I'll show you how they would look together in a competition sequence.

Aresti Symbols Primer

Once you get used to the definitions for a few Aresti schematics, you'll probably agree that glancing at a sequence defined by them is much easier than reading descriptions. It'll be like glancing at a map to find your way, an important tool during a fast-moving, complex aerobatic competition sequence.

The purpose of this section is to explain what Aresti symbols are describing. There are many such symbols for multitudes of aerobatic maneuvers, many of which you might not have heard of. But if you understand the basic symbols, you'll be able to decipher a required aerobatic maneuver or sequence.

Sequences for each level of competition—Primary, Sportsman, Intermediate, Advanced— are periodically changed for a new season of competition contests. You can obtain the current year's sequences from the International Aerobatic Club (IAC).

Let's start with the easiest symbol…

Normal Flight

This depicts straight and level normal flight. The dot at the beginning of the line shows the entry to the maneuver, and the perpendicular line at the end (cap line) signifies the conclusion.

Inverted Flight

The inverted normal flight symbol is similar, except it's shown as a dashed line.

Spin (one turn)

Spins are shown as a right triangle (one corner is 90°) embedded within the downline. The small number above the entry dot shows the number of rotations.

Loop

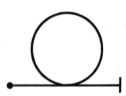

This symbol of a normal loop speaks for itself, nice and round, not egg shaped.

Slow Roll

The slow roll symbol is also easy to decipher. When the arced arrow goes through the line, it signifies one roll. If the arc begins at the line, it is a half roll. Other fractions of a roll (i.e., ¼) are signified with the fraction shown at the arrow's point. The direction of flight is always into the concave portion of the arc (from left to right in this example). The arrow does not show the direction of the roll, which is the choice of the pilot. By the way, slow rolls are commonly seen in competition, but aileron rolls are not. The aileron roll is presented in this training curriculum as a relatively easy building-block maneuver.

Slow Roll with 2 hesitations ("points")

The little "2" at the end of the arrow shows how many pauses during the slow roll, including at the starting attitude. This one shows a brief stop inverted before returning to ordinary flight. If the number was "4" it would be a four-point roll.

Immelmann

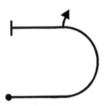

The half-loop figure is easy to understand, but the short roll arrow sticking out of the top signifies a continuous half-roll after passing through inverted, and ending right-side up. Notice that the half-roll arc begins on the line, not through it.

Barrel Roll

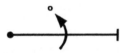

The little O-shape at the end of the arrow signifies a barrel roll. You probably won't see barrel rolls in a competition sequence, but they are common for recreational aerobatics, and variations of it are used in military tactical operations.

Snap Roll

Here's that "spin" triangle again, but it's an isosceles (two equal sides) triangle this time. If the triangle crosses the flight line, it's a full rotation snap roll. If it does not cross the line, it's a half snap roll. If the triangle is a solid color, it's an outside snap roll.

Avalanche

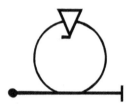

A single complete snap roll on the top of a loop.

Split S

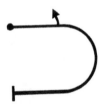

Here's another half-loop, but notice that it starts as straight and level flight at the top (indicated by the entry dot). The half-roll arrow shows that you roll inverted before pulling through the back half of the loop to upright. The split-S symbol doesn't tell you to slow WAY down before pulling through the back of the loop, but you know that, right?

Cuban 8

Notice how this shows where the Cuban 8's loop starts and ends. Also notice how the half-arrows show half-rolls from inverted.

Reverse Cuban 8

Look carefully to see the Cuban starting with a 45° upline, a half-roll to inverted, a loop, and doing it all over again. A lot of information packed into a simple-looking schematic.

Hammerhead

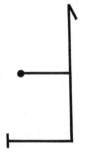

All the lines are straight to show the hammerhead. Note the angled line at the top to signify a vertical direction reversal. Also notice that the downline is longer than the upline, accounting for gravitational effects.

Humpty Bump

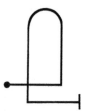

Notice that the half-loop is only the top half, and it should be constant radius throughout the arc. The other two humpty pulling actions (pull to vertical upline, pull to normal flight) should be made at a higher G-load to make it a 90° angle.

Primary Level Sequence Schematic

Let's put a few of those Aristi symbols together into a sequence. See if you can identify the maneuvers in this Primary sequence from the International Aerobatic Club's 2020 competition season. (Maneuver descriptions will follow the schematic.)

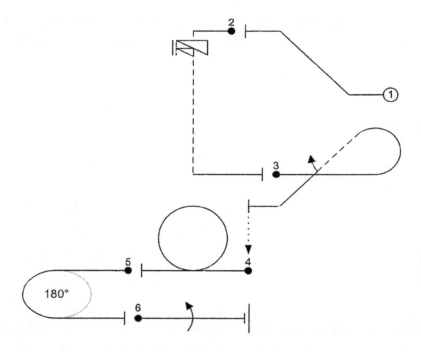

6 Maneuvers: 45° upline > 2-turn spin > half Cuban 8 > loop > 180° turn > slow roll.

Part 3
Controlling Upsets

Tale Spins   *By Arland Nau*

"Let's see...do I push or pull to go up or down when right-side up or upside down?"

Chapter 5
Introduction to Upset Recoveries

Upset Flight Training Procedures

When I act as a flight instructor for upset training flights, I explain each loss of control (LOC) scenario in the lesson plan to my student, and then discuss a recommended recovery procedure. In the air, I'll again describe each LOC event and review the recovery procedure before setting it up.

Avoiding vertigo

Unlike with non-aerobatic "unusual attitude" recovery training, I will not ask the student to look down or close his eyes when I am setting up the upset. This would predictably cause vertigo, and does not simulate a realistic situation. Awareness of the setup, in fact, lets the student experience a chain of factors that can evolve into an airplane's loss of control. When you can identify those factors, it helps you recognize and prevent an imminent LOC.

Student participation

Sometimes I will put a student into a "risky" situation (although at an altitude high enough to not be risky). At the point of LOC, I'll ask the student to take over and recover. Usually, though, I let the student handle the controls from beginning to end of each upset setup, and I let the student cause the loss of control incident and make the recovery. After the student recovers (or fails to), I'll ask her to critique her performance. After that, I'll comment on her critique and add my thoughts.

Teaching moments

The best time to learn from an experience is during or immediately after having that experience. Sometimes that learning opportunity arises during aerobatic maneuvers, like the following examples.

- If I feel the wings burble at the top of a loop, I'll ask the student during or afterward if she felt the beginning of a stall. If she didn't, she will likely be more aware of the momentum energy needed at the top of the loop, and will likely be more sensitive to any wing wobbling. As a remedial exercise, I might even set up a large, low-G loop to recreate an impending stall, and give the student a chance to abort the maneuver.

- On the downside of a hammerhead, I sometimes feel the wings start to stall because the student is pulling out of the downline too soon and/or too aggressively, maybe even while the controls are still uncoordinated. Giving the student feedback about that incipient stall or imminent spin makes him more aware of his control inputs.

- When the ailerons or elevator respond sluggishly to control inputs, I'll ask the student if he knows the wings are partially stalled, or are on the edge of a stall. The idea is to learn that sluggish control responses—in any attitude—can signal an immanent stall or spin.

- At the top of a two-point slow roll, sometimes a student lets the nose drop down too far, resulting in a pronounced inverted dive. As the nose passes through the horizon, I'm quick to remind her to "*push-and-roll, push-and-roll*" before she gets a chance to pull us into a hasty, instinctive split-S, a mistake that could overspeed and over-stress the airplane and pilot, and lose LOTS of altitude.

- Every once in a while, a student will inadvertently push us into an outside spin at the conclusion of an Immelmann, or more commonly, after the apogee of a hammerhead turn. If they don't immediately recognize the upset, or they haven't had outside spin recovery training yet, I'll say "*I've got the controls*," and I'll recover. I take over because recovery from an outside spin is counter-intuitive without training, and it's too erratic and rapid to talk the untrained student through it. It's still a great teaching moment, though, because afterward the student is highly motivated to learn how to recover from outside spins.

How aerobatic skills reduce errors

I'm always glad when those inadvertent errors happen with me in the cockpit. Afterward, we'll talk about why the upset happened, how it could have been prevented, how it could have been recognized, and the proper recovery procedure. But these learning hiccups seldom happen during my training flights because my curriculum builds one skill upon another, and the student gradually becomes competent enough to learn the next maneuver without mishaps. By the time they get to more complex aerobatic maneuvers or the extreme attitude upset scenarios that I will soon describe, they should be skilled enough to detect and manage sustained stalls, multi-turn spins, and unintended inverted dives.

Monitor your best learning rate

Practicing upset maneuvers can be mentally and physically taxing, so you might not want to do them all in one flight lesson. This curriculum groups maneuvers into lessons that create an effective and efficient learning progression, but that does not mean that all the listed maneuvers have to be squeezed into a single training flight. Learn at your best pace, no matter what pace that is, and then you'll learn optimally. If a flight lesson stops being fun or exciting, it's time to declare the flight lesson a success and return to the airport. Quality always trumps quantity when it comes to flight training.

The most dangerous upsets

According to statistics periodically gathered in the Joseph T. Nall Report—which is available at the Aircraft Owners and Pilots Association (AOPA) website—the most dangerous, frequent, and lethal upsets involved stalls that degraded into spins, usually close to the ground. For that reason, many of the upset scenarios in this curriculum will require stall/spin recoveries, sometimes from quick breaks into spins from extreme attitudes.

Chapter 6
Loss of Control During Aerobatic Practice

This chapter is devoted to recovering from loss of control (LOC) errors during aerobatic maneuvers. A variety of common maneuvers and error scenarios will be discussed with the intention of practicing those recoveries later with a competent aerobatic flight instructor.

1. Pinched Looping Maneuvers

Stalling during a looping maneuver (i.e., loop, cloverleaf, avalanche, barrel roll, Immelmann, Cuban 8) might seem unlikely, but with low speeds while inverted on top, and high angles of attack on the backside, conditions are ripe for a potential inadvertent stall or spin. Pulling too hard or too fast with low airspeed and high angle of attack (i.e., "pinching" the maneuver) at any point in a looping maneuver can set things off. Recovery will require quick recognition and action, and enough altitude for a safe recovery. Unrecoverable stalls from looping maneuvers close to the ground have been a leading cause of airshow crashes, often fatal—always to the horror of spectators.

As you know by now, if a stall happens, pulling harder only deepens the stall. Add a bit of yaw, and you could trigger a spin. And if a stall or spin takes you by surprise, especially with the nose pointed down, your first instinct might be to pull harder. If a spin develops somewhere during the loop, it would make the recovery all the more complex, which is why you learned the avalanche earlier in this curriculum.

If you have plenty of altitude, you'll have no problem as a trained aerobatic pilot in reducing the angle of attack, whether on the upline after initial pullup, over top while inverted, or on the downline on the backside. Let's look at each of these.

For these looping maneuver recoveries, note your entry altitude, which should be higher than for normal loop practice, and then note it again when you've completed the recovery to determine the amount of lost altitude. Let's look at some typical scenarios. (I don't think

I have to remind you at this point to make thorough clearing turns before every setup, but I'll remind you anyway.)

A. Imminent Stall During Pullup into a Loop

The setup. Start your pullup up into a loop with less airspeed and backpressure than you normally enter with.

The upset. When you are almost perpendicular to the horizon, assume that you won't have enough power or momentum to finish the loop.

The recovery. Abandon the maneuver by pointing the nose down and recovering from the dive. The quickest way to nose over will be using full rudder to yaw over, like a mushy hammerhead. If you pull the stick back as with a humpty bump, you might stall due to insufficient airspeed, excessive angle of attack, and lack of momentum. If you try to pitch the nose forward to recover, you'll feel negative Gs.

B. Stalling on Top of a Loop

If you pull too hard while inverted, you could stall while upside down. The nose will eventually drop toward the earth, but if you keep holding the stick back, it could sustain the stall, even though you are pointed downward.

The setup. Enter a low G, lackluster pullup for a big fat loop, and add forward stick when rounding the top.

The upset. When the wings shudder, signaling they are about ready to stall with negative angle of attack, that will be your recovery signal.

The recovery. Gently ease back on the stick to lower the nose and pick up speed. When enough airspeed develops, either continue the ill-shaped loop, or abandon it by rolling out while pushing on the stick, then pull out of your right-side up dive. But push and pull carefully because you don't want to trigger a stall or spin.

If you did trigger either an inside or outside spin, recover the way you have been practicing earlier in this curriculum.

You might prefer to abort the maneuver because it will save time and altitude by abandoning an already lousy loop. (Your Immelmann skills will help you with this alternative recovery.)

Note the amount of altitude lost after each of these recoveries. That's at least how high above the ground you needed to be in order to recover safely.

C. Stalling on a Backside of a Loop

The setup. Enter a big sluggish loop and prolong the inverted portion on top.

The upset. When the airspeed begins to peter out on top, begin to head downward while pulling hard enough on the stick to feel the elevator response getting sluggish, or enough to feel a stall. This will be the signal to prevent a stall.

The recovery. Ease off the stick backpressure enough to regain some airspeed and reduce the angle of attack. When the stick feels responsive, complete the loop.

2. Imminent Tail Slide

The setup. To simulate an imminent tail slide during a hammerhead, dive to pick up the recommended entry speed, and then pull up into a vertical upline.

The upset. As soon as the nose is straight upward, assume you've exhausted your forward momentum.

The recovery. Push either rudder full in, and after regaining some airspeed energy on the downline, pull out of the dive. Don't worry about whether it was a correct hammerhead. The objective was to avoid a tail slide.

Alternative recovery. We'll do this again, but you'll recover with full back pressure this time. If you were in a real tail slide, the nose will aggressively pitch forward with backpressure on the stick, but don't let your upline last that long. In this simulation, the airplane will flop over on its back with backpressure on the stick, and then point into a downline dive. This pullback is sort of a sloppy humpty bump, something you've already learned. If you were especially slow before starting the recovery, the nose might pendulum a little while you regain airspeed.

During either of these recoveries, make sure your airspeed picks up on the downline sufficiently before pulling out of the dive. Otherwise, you could stall even though you are pointing toward Mother Earth.

3. Imminent Outside Stall

The setup. To practice preventing an outside stall (entered from pushing the stick), bring the power to idle, roll the airplane inverted and keep the stick going forward enough to maintain altitude.

The upset. When the airflow over the wings begins to burble, start your recovery.

The recovery. Ease back on the forward stick pressure enough to let the nose drop down just below the horizon, thereby preventing a full stall. When airspeed picks up, push the stick forward enough to prevent the inverted dive from steepening while rolling out, and then pull the airplane out of the resulting upright dive (This *push-and-roll* recovery should be your intuitive response to inverted dives by now).

4. Unintended Outside Spin

The setup. Half-loop into an Immelmann, and bring the power to idle. Keep the stick going forward enough to maintain altitude.

The upset. Keep increasing forward pressure until the airplane stalls, push one of the rudders full in and add full forward pressure, making the airplane break into an outside spin.

The recovery. As soon as the airplane begins to spin, touch the throttle and say "Idle" aloud, (to simulated reducing power to idle) all the while neutralizing the ailerons and applying full opposite rudder. When the rotation slows or stops, bring the stick back past neutral. After recovering from the resulting dive, return the airplane to normal flight.

Chapter 7
Loss of Control During Normal Operations

It's a nice sunny day. Severe clear... wind calm. Your engine is placidly humming along.

How could anything possibly go wrong?

Having an airplane unexpectedly go out of control is not limited to aerobatic operations. The loss of control (LOC) scenarios in this chapter will help you appreciate how a series of minor errors can link together into a dangerous chain reaction. You'll also see the advantage of having at least some basic aerobatic skills to help you recover quickly, and with minimum altitude loss. Besides learning how to recover expediently in an actual LOC upset, the skills you learn in this chapter will help you become sensitized to factors that can lead to a LOC.

Stalls and spins at low levels

It troubles me deeply that so many pilots continue to lose control of their airplanes from stalling or spinning, sometimes while in the airport pattern, and sometimes while buzzing or while taking photos at low levels. Next to flying into bad weather, these stall and spin incidents are statistically the greatest life-threatening hazard to general aviation pilots and their passengers.

An unintended accelerated spin seems to happen instantaneously, and develops when a cross controlled wing is abruptly pulled or pushed beyond critical angle of attack. (Think snap roll.) It might be impossible for anyone to recover from an accelerated spin at pattern altitude, but I believe that stall/spin training and practice can sharpen your awareness of factors that can lead to stalls and spins during normal operations. And remember, an airplane has to stall before it can spin—prevent the stall, prevent the spin. Also remember that increasing your bank increases the G load, which increases your stall speed.

Closely monitoring your airspeed when flying at low altitude is a critical life-saver. Stall warning alarms and angle of attack indicators also aid your situational awareness. Here are some other early warning factors that aerobatic training and upset training can help you become sensitive to.

- **Sluggish control responses.** The lower the airspeed, the less air is flowing over the control surfaces, and the less control responsiveness you'll feel with your hands, arms, and feet. Your aerobatic and stall/spin flight experience can help you be on high alert when controls feel less responsive.

- **Uncoordinated flight.** Beginning with simple Dutch rolls and aileron rolls early in your aerobatic flight training with this curriculum, you became increasingly aware of uncoordinated yawing sensations. A skid pushes your body away from the turn, a slip pulls your body into the turn. That kinesthetic feedback is a useful indicator when your eyes are busy watching something other than the inclinometer (i.e., the "ball")—but do glance at the ball when you are able.

- **Hazardous flight attitude combination.** I hope your nerve endings stand on end whenever you are at low altitude and you tighten or steepen your bank, especially if you are cross-controlled and your airspeed is decreasing. That's a recipe for an alarmingly robust accelerated stall/spin that you might not have enough altitude to recover from. A preventative measure at low level would be to keep all turns coordinated, make shallow or medium banks, and keep your airspeed well above stall speed. An added safety measure would be to avoid unnecessary low-level operations. For example, take your photos from a safely-high altitude, and then crop them when you get back on the ground. Or, instead of buzzing your friend's house, call him from your smartphone and tell him to come out and wave because you are circling from a safe, non-annoying altitude.

- **Wing and airframe flutter.** If your stall warning horn fails, you still might be able to feel an imminent stall by the flutter in your stick or the seat of your pants. Most aerobatic trainers are designed with wing "washout," giving the root of the wing a slightly higher angle of incidence. That design makes a stall develop gradually, starting at the root, which alerts you while your ailerons still have enough control authority to maneuver. Some advanced aerobatic airplanes, however, have little or no washout because they are designed to enter stall and spin maneuvers on demand, without delay.

Denial of indicators

Pilots sometimes ignore the above indicators, as if denying their significance. Psychologists call that reaction *post cognitive dissonance* (PCD), which means that if what you see or feel is contrary to what you expect or believe should be happening, you might ignore the reality and fail to react. You are especially vulnerable to PCD blocking out unexpected indicators when you are concentrating on a ground reference or a precision maneuver. PCD can also happen when pilots discount the significance of unexpected marginal weather.

Simulating the scenarios

Here are common low-level scenarios that can sometimes lead to what is officiously described as *uncontrolled flight into terrain*. You should simulate these scenarios, of course, at a safe altitude, and with a competent aerobatic flight instructor.

1. Loss of Power During Climb Out

The setup. At a safe altitude at which you would practice spins, imagine you've just taken off with trees at the end of the runway, so you are climbing at "best angle" airspeed (V_x).

The upset. You simulate having just passed over the trees at the end of the runway when your instructor brings the throttle to idle to simulate your engine stopping.

The recovery. Push on the stick enough to avoid stalling because the angle of attack is increasing rapidly. Maintain best glide speed and look ahead for a place to land.

Alternate Loss of Power Recovery During Climb Out

Attempting to Turn and Land at the Airport.

When experimenting from a safe altitude, I've been able to successfully simulate turning back to an imaginary airport and making a safe landing, but the variable factors include the aircraft's performance limitations, the pilot's reaction time and control inputs, the loss-of-power altitude, and the wind speed and direction. Try the following experiment at a safe altitude in your airplane.

The setup. Repeat the above loss-of-power simulation at a safe altitude and over a straight landmark such as a road, but this time note your beginning altitude.

The upset. When the throttle is brought to idle, wait 3 or 4 seconds to simulate being taken by surprise.

The recovery. Immediately roll left into a coordinated 45° bank (the bank angle that gives you equal horizontal and vertical lift) while maintaining your airplane's best glide speed. Turn 220° or so, (turning only 180° will put you parallel with the runway instead back over the centerline). Once over the straight landmark (simulating the runway center line), turn to line up with the downwind imaginary runway. Check your altitude loss. Did you make it back high enough to land on the runway?

Experiment with other turnaround factors. Have some fun and expand your recovery repertoire by changing the below factors and keeping track of your results. You will be pushing the aerodynamic limits of your airplane, so be on high alert for stall/spin conditions.

1. Try carefully lowering your turnaround glide speed just below best angle of climb (V_x).
   Try different bank angles, but make sure your turns are coordinated.
2. If you had crosswind from the right during your simulated take off, make your return bank to the right into the wind to stay closer to the runway.

Caution #1 - If the runway headwind is brisk on take off, you'll risk using a lot of runway with high groundspeed for the tailwind return. In that situation, it might be safer to look ahead for the best landing spot when you lose power. (I've had three engine failures during my years of flying—two on short final, one during a multi-turn spin)—so I'm always looking for landing spots, especially after take off. At my home base airport, I already have landing spots picked for both directions off all three runways.

Caution #2 – A pilot friend of mine had an actual power failure during climb out, just after taking off, and he used full rudder to yaw the nose around while keeping the wings level with ailerons. I don't know what his engine-out altitude was, but he successfully landed downwind on a taxiway parallel to the runway. I simulated that procedure at a safe altitude, and did not find it superior to the recoveries discussed above. A low airspeed yaw like that also risks a snapped spin, which could be unrecoverable at low altitude.

2. Stall/Spin During Climb Out

Picture this: you are taking off on a hot day, loaded to gross weight. You roll left into a climbing 45° banked cross-wind leg, pulling on the stick to maintain best angle of climb speed (V_x), while still pushing on the right rudder for adverse yaw, harder than necessary during a left turn. At this point in your training, you should recognize this slow-speed slip as a potential stall and spin setup. Not only that, but when the spin breaks (begins), it will be to the side where your rudder is being pushed, opposite of the direction of the turn. The nose will pitch up dramatically, roll you to the other side, and then point toward the ground.

Set this practice up at normal spin practice altitude, but keep track of your recovery altitude loss by first noting your entry altitude. After recovering, note your altitude again to see if you would have survived from pattern altitude.

The setup. Reduce power to idle (to tame the stall/spin break) and maintain your altitude by pulling back on the stick. When the airspeed reaches best angle of climb speed, roll into a 45° bank to a cross-wind heading.

The upset. While turning, pull stick full back and add full rudder to the opposite side of the turn.

The recovery. Recover as soon as the nose rolls up over the top and into an incipient (beginning) spin.

After recovery, check the altitude loss to see if you would have survived. If this happened with full power in an actual climb-out, the airplane's break into a spin would have been even more dramatic. This simulation should make you forever-after on high alert for factors that can inadvertently and suddenly stall and spin the airplane during the take off and departure climb-out.

3. Stall/Spin During Approach to Landing

Again, at a safe spin practice altitude, we'll assume an imaginary airport's pattern elevation is 1,000 feet. Use a road or some other ground reference to simulate the runway. If your airplane has flaps, do not use them in this simulation. (See your airplane's pilot operating handbook for instructions about stall recoveries with the flaps extended.)

The setup. At pattern altitude on the downwind leg, reduce power to idle and slow to landing speed. Turn left to a final approach from the base leg while at landing speed, but assume you rolled out past the glide path to the runway. Make a shallow bank to attempt a return to the final approach, and then push the left rudder to yaw the nose over, all the while pulling the stick back to reduce speed.

The upset. At the first sign of a stall, still holding left rudder, abruptly pull full back on the stick (which is a predictable panicked response when the nose pitches down from a stall, especially at low level). Instead of rolling up over the top as with the previously described climb-out slip, the skidding airplane's nose will tuck down into a spin.

The recovery. Make a normal spin recovery. Check the exit altitude to see if you would have survived.

As with the take-off spin simulation, this exercise is largely to make you super-vigilant about airspeed, angle of bank, and coordinated control inputs while in the pattern.

If your final approach isn't right in a real-life situation, make a short safety timeout to go around.

4. Go Around

You go around as a safety measure, so make sure the go around itself is done safely. You should practice solo go-arounds regularly, and have them critiqued by a flight instructor during flight reviews.

The setup. If you are practicing solo, I recommend simulating the go around a safe altitude away from an airport. For this simulation, assume the pattern elevation is 1,000 feet above the runway. If you practice at an actual towered airport, advise the tower controllers ahead of time about your intention to practice a go around. If at a non-towered airport, announce your intention to make a go-around over the Common Traffic Advisory Frequency (CTAF), but don't trust that all nearby pilots are listening, or even have a radio. If your airplane has carburetor heat, pull carb heat normally to prepare for the landing, and push it back in when you need full power, unless the airplane's POH recommends a different procedure. Make a normal approach to a landing at landing airspeed. Extend the flaps if they are normally used in landings.

The upset. During short final approach (simulated at altitude or actual), assume another airplane has pulled out onto the runway for a take off.

The recovery. Add full power and push the carb heat off (if applicable) while pushing on the stick to maintain your altitude and gain airspeed. (If you have flaps down, gradually and incrementally retract them while bringing the stick back as needed to maintain a safe airspeed and altitude.) When flaps are fully retracted and you reach best angle of climb airspeed (V_x), climb back to pattern altitude with that airspeed.

Note: Before practicing go arounds, consult your airplane's pilots operating handbook (POH), and adhere to the manufacturer's recommended procedures.

5. Stall/Spin During Low-Level Operations

Aerial photography at low level is dangerous because you are distracted by multi-tasking between the airplane and the camera, increased angles of attack, higher wing loading, and lower airspeeds. Turning repeatedly while watching something on the ground is a recipe for dizzying vertigo, for both pilot and passenger. Coupled with this fearsome mix, the low altitude would make an accelerated stall or spin difficult at best—impossible at worse—to recover from.

Even if you aren't the photographer, it's easy as the pilot to get absorbed with rolling, turning, and slipping the airplane to compose the photographic subject, trying to keep it in sight while getting the best light and composition, all the while not noticing that the airplane's attitude has become uncoordinated, the airspeed dangerously low, and the bank perilously steep.

Buzzing presents a slightly different hazard. Imagine gliding with reduced power toward someone's house, then adding full power over the rooftop while climbing steeply, rocking the wings, and looking back to see if anyone on the ground is waving. In the meantime, the wings are loading up, angle of attack is increasing, and the airspeed is decreasing. At this point, that should be a familiar setup for disaster, and you should respect the possible dire consequences for that brief showoff thrill.

But to truly appreciate a low-level operation mishap, let's experience one.

The setup. To stage a simulation, start at your normal spin practice altitude. We'll pretend that altitude is 500 feet above the ground. Reduce the power to idle and start a 45° bank, bringing the stick back to maintain altitude.

The upset. When the speed is about halfway between stall speed and snap roll entry speed, pull the stick fully back and add full rudder opposite of the turn direction to snap the airplane into a spin.

The recovery. Start recovering as soon as you break into either a stall or spin. After recovering, check your altimeter to see how much altitude you lost. I can tell you right now that you probably regained control of the airplane below your simulated "ground" level. It's a great lesson that hopefully will stay with you throughout your flying years.

Photo safety tips

I take photos at a safe altitude and simply crop the images later to make the perspective look as low as I want it to. That way, I can control the composition and touch up the lighting and color saturation later, while safely on the ground. Regardless of the altitude, however, I know that circling around a photo subject on the ground (i.e., my passenger's house) can cause my passenger to have vertigo, perhaps severe enough to make him sick. The recipe for generating this sickening dizziness is looking out the side window at something on the ground while repeatedly turning around it. It drives the semicircular canals nuts and they send a complaint directly to the brain. Instead, I maintain a safe altitude and slip the airplane to maintain a straight line, and then tell my photographing passenger to take his shots. I have him look up when I roll out and turn the corner. In other words, I make a box around my photo subject instead of a circle. My passenger only looks down when the airplane is slipped into a straight path. I only recommend this to aerobatic-trained pilots because the airplane could still stall or spin. Remember, stay high and you'll be safe.

Buzzing safety tips

Don't ever buzz anything or anyone, anywhere, at any time. It's dangerous, it makes you seem like a showoff, it annoys and scares the neighbors, it makes general aviation pilots seem irresponsible, and it might be illegal. If you want to get someone's attention while you are flying over their house, stay at a safe altitude and call them on your mobile phone. If they want to come out and wave, they'll certainly be able to see you, even if you're a couple of thousand feet AGL.

6. Turning 180° After Entering IMC

Getting caught in instrument weather conditions hopefully won't require an aerobatic-style upset recovery, but since flying unintendedly into instrument meteorological conditions (IMC) is the number one source of general aviation pilot (and passenger) fatalities, we should treat it as a dangerous upset. This should be the same exercise you would make during a proper flight review, but you should practice the simulation described below with a safety pilot more often than once every two years.

The best IMC survival tip

The best way to survive an IMC incident is to prevent it. Make your go/no-go decision based on stone-cold logic: Am I taking a risk to get there on time? Am I trying to avoid disappointing my passengers? Am I afraid of seeming overly-cautious, inexperienced, or afraid? What's the worst thing that can happen if I delay or don't go?

If you face potential icing conditions, low clouds, or reduced visibility, another influencing factor might be the human tendency to deny the reality or seriousness of those dangers (see "post cognitive dissidence," discussed earlier). If you have any doubt while enroute, gather the gumption to turn back, or land at the nearest airport and wait for better weather. That was standard procedure for the early barnstormers and airmail pilots (the ones who survived), and it should be your standard too. Our modern culture is fueled by haste and speed, but you and your airplane are still subject to the forces of nature, so don't gamble your life and the lives of passengers to try to get somewhere ASAP in marginal weather.

As a personal aside, many years ago I got caught in icing conditions immediately after taking off into special VFR conditions with a Cessna 150. The flight school I was instructing for always sent one of the CFIs up in marginal weather to check the conditions before letting students practice in the pattern. I started picking up ice when I circled back to land, but by the time I was on final approach my windshield was completely iced over, and I had to open and look out the side window to land. After taxiing back to the school's ramp, I found about a quarter inch of ice on the wings. Go/no-go decisions have been relatively easy for me after that. If in doubt, I reschedule the flight. If enroute, I make a 180 and monitor nearest airports on my GPS.

That's my lecture on avoiding IMC. Now let's look at how to recover if you find yourself flying into worsening scud.

The setup. Fly straight and level at a safe altitude with a flight instructor or safety pilot. Your safety pilot's job will be to watch for traffic.

The upset. Put on your instrument practice hood or frosted goggles to simulate entering IMC.

The recovery. Note your compass heading and turn left (because you probably turn that way most often) with a 2-minute standard turn rate. Roll out when you reach a heading 180° from your entry heading. After a minute or two of straight and level flight, remove your hood or goggles.

Optional IMC recovery simulations

1. Assume that you flew into icing conditions. After rolling out on your 180° heading, glide down 500 feet into warmer air before removing your hood or goggles.
2. After rolling out on your 180° heading, use a simple radar app to determine the shortest heading to avoid or fly out of precipitation, or simulate calling Flight Service for assistance (simulate by talking to your instructor or safety pilot on the intercom).
3. After you roll out on your 180° heading, remove your hood or goggles and find the nearest airport, using a paper chart, an electronic map app, your GPS navigation software, or in the absence of those, try your smartphone map. Whichever system you are relying on, turn to a heading to that nearest airport.

Abbreviated Extreme Attitude and Upset Syllabuses

I suggest the following syllabus for pilots who are on a strict budget or with time limitations. I would want any pilot to have the chance to learn basic upset recoveries. As with the full-course syllabus in this book, you should exercise due diligence to make sure your certified flight instructor is competent to teach aerobatics and spins, and make sure the aircraft you train in is designed for aerobatic flight.

Lesson plans for the below maneuvers, as well as the upset "setups" are the same as those found in the full-curriculum lesson plans found in this book, and the upset maneuvers described later in Part 3.

Abbreviated syllabus

This abbreviated syllabus is intended to introduce pilots to upset recoveries, but is not intended to prepare pilots to practice aerobatics without an instructor. To become competent enough to safely fly aerobatics solo, I recommend that pilots receive training in underlying fundamentals (for example, learning loops and rolls before learning barrel rolls).

Upset setups

In addition to learning underlying fundamentals, pilots should learn how to recover from aerobatic upsets and how to abort maneuvers that cannot be completed safely (i.e., excessive speed on a downline). **These upset scenarios will be described shortly in Part 3.**

5-Hour Extreme Attitude and Upset Recovery Syllabus

Lesson 1 – Basic Stick and Rudder Skills Review

- Dutch Rolls
- Minimum Controllable Airspeed
- Sustained Stall
- 60° Banked Turns (both directions)

Lesson 2 – Primary Aerobatic Maneuvers

- Aileron Roll
- Loop
- 2-Point Aileron Roll

Lesson 3 – Combination Maneuver and Spin Intro

- Loop With an Aileron Roll at the End
- ½ Turn Spins (both directions)

Lesson 4 – Developed Spin Upset Recoveries

- Full Turn Spins (both directions)
- Normal Operation Upset Recoveries (Part 3, Setups 1-3)

Lesson 5 – Inverted Dive and Upsets Continued

- Inverted Dive Recovery
- Normal Operation Upset Recoveries (Part 3, Setups 4-6)

3-Hour Upset-Only Recovery Syllabus

Lesson 1 – Basic stick and Rudder Skills Review

- Dutch Rolls
- Minimum Controllable Airspeed
- Sustained Stall
- 60° Banked Turn (both directions)

Lesson 2 – Phase 1 Upset Recoveries

- ½ Turn Spins (both directions)
- Normal Operation Upset Recoveries (Part 3, Setups 1-3)

Lesson 3 – Phase 2 Upset Recoveries

- Full Turn Spins (both directions)
- Normal Operation Upset Recoveries (Part 3, Setups 4-6)

My Departing Wing Waggle

This concludes my shared experiences and musings about learning, practicing, and teaching aerobatics. If you haven't already found a competent aerobatic flight instructor, you could contact the International Aerobatic Club for a list of members who are aerobatic certified flight instructors. You will have to do your own due diligence to determine whether a particular individual's competence, background, and aerobatic experience is appropriate for you.

During my early aerobatic years, I traveled from my home in Minnesota to Florida, Texas, and California to get advanced aerobatic and spin training from outstanding flight instructors. I had a lot of fun, and I encourage you to make an investment of time and money for a few days of training that you'll never forget or regret.

You've probably noticed that my favorite aviation themes are fun, learning, and safety. I think that's what general aviation should be all about. I wish you many fun hours of safe flying and happy landings.

Jim Luger, CFI

Minnetonka, Minnesota

*You may download this book's flight syllabus, see updates, and share your thoughts with me at **JamesLuger.com***

Maneuver Index

Jim Luger has been teaching aerobatics as a certified flight instructor for over 50 years. He holds a commercial pilot certificate, with ratings for seaplane, instrument, and multi-engine. Jim is a recipient of the FAA's highest pilot tribute, the Wright Brothers Master Pilot Award. He is also a Certified Distance Education Instructor (CDEI). Jim lives with his wife Judy in Minnetonka, Minnesota, and his aviation base is nearby Flying Cloud Airport, where he is aerobatic instructor for the 12 Kilo Delta Flying Club.

The illustrations within the book were created by Arland Nau.

You'll find a free download of this book's **Aerobatic Flight Syllabus and Log** at **james.luger.com**

CPSIA information can be obtained
at www.ICGtesting.com
Printed in the USA
LVHW060716180620
658104LV00003B/75